The
Determining
Factor

Robert C. Bucknell

THE DETERMINING FACTOR

iUniverse books may be ordered through booksellers or by contacting:

iUniverse
1663 Liberty Drive
Bloomington, IN 47403
www.iuniverse.com
1-800-Authors (1-800-288-4677)

Because of the dynamic nature of the Internet, any web addresses or links contained in this book may have changed since publication and may no longer be valid. The views expressed in this work are solely those of the author and do not necessarily reflect the views of the publisher, and the publisher hereby disclaims any responsibility for them.

Any people depicted in stock imagery provided by Thinkstock are models, and such images are being used for illustrative purposes only. Certain stock imagery © Thinkstock.

ISBN: 978-1-5320-0461-2 (sc)
ISBN: 978-1-5320-0460-5 (e)

Library of Congress Control Number: 2016916666

Print information available on the last page.

iUniverse rev. date: 11/03/2016

Robert Bucknell has authored two books: His first work, "Embrace the Truth – Prophecy Revealed through Current Events", covered issues from a prophetical viewpoint, pertinent to the date of actual printing, back in 1996. This first work opened the eyes of many concerning things they once held in restraint for lack of understanding truth.

This current work expands on those very same issues, showing how intricately and accurately God's Prophetic Word has truly proven itself since his first writing. It presents in laymen's terms, the complex issues of today, and how many of the problems plaguing the world in our generation have been prophesied; while he clearly outlines what must be done, and how to avoid the consequences of man's foolishness.

His purpose in writing this book is to help one understand God and His plan for mankind, and the great hope that awaits those who are willing to listen to what God has to say to our generation.

This Book is Dedicated to:

Jesus Christ

One day this body will turn
to dust; yet will I live through
the Blood of
Christ Jesus
My Savior

Surely I came into this
world with nothing
and henceforth
shall I return ... Yet
The Glory of Eternal Life
with Him shall be mine!

CONTENTS

PREFACE

IT DOESN'T TAKE GENIUS to understand that mankind is confronted by very real and complex problems. We need to ask ourselves: "Do men comprehend what significance all these problems represent in today's generation?" Do we truly realize what lies just ahead of us? We can no longer hide the truth by burying our heads in the sand.

I have undertaken a tremendous leap of faith in bringing this work to you because, although I have a college education, and although I have been prudently studying and researching the Scriptures (the Holy Bible) for more than fifty years, I do not have the usual type credentials of a scholar to give authority to this work. However, please consider the following words found in II Timothy 2:15 KJV:

> "Study to show thyself approved unto God, a workman that needeth not to be ashamed, rightly dividing the word of truth".

> "I thank thee, O Father, Lord of heaven and earth, because Thou hast hid these things from the wise and prudent, and hast <u>revealed them unto babes</u>. Even so, Father; for it seemed good in Thy sight". (Matthew 11:25-27 KJV).

God's Word has been revealed to both scholars and non-scholars alike. His Word is not for the self-proclaimed 'wise and prudent' types, but for 'babes'; meaning those who have opened up their hearts so that God can reveal Himself and His truths to them.

One of the greatest scientists the world has ever known was Sir Isaac Newton. He believed that the Bible is truly the unerring Word of God and he made the following remarkable statement:

> "About the time of the end, a body of men will be raised up who will turn their attention to the prophesies and insist upon their literal interpretation in the midst of much clamor and opposition".

This thought is confirmed in God's Word where the Lord told Daniel, the prophet, to write:

> "But thou, O Daniel, shut up the words, and seal the book, even to the time of the end: many shall run to and fro, and <u>knowledge shall be increased</u>". (Daniel 12:4) (Underscore mine).

If you'll notice, Sir Isaac Newton stated that, *'a body of men will be raised up . . .'*. He was astute enough to realize that this *'body of men'* would not necessarily consist of theologians, scholars, and scientists; but they would include many ordinary men moved by God's Spirit (like was the case with most of Jesus' disciples); for God does use the *"lowly to confound the wise". (I Corinthians 1:27 KJV).*

And, as Daniel wrote, it will not be until the 'End Times', when travel will be worldwide, (many will run to and fro), and 'Knowledge shall increase', (at a time when people everywhere will understand things that were, in the past, seemingly impossible to comprehend).

My purpose is to help you understand how God works and that one does not necessarily have to be scholarly to understand God's Word. Each and every one of us can allow God's Word to touch our hearts simply by letting God's Spirit work within us. This is brought to light in the following verse of Scripture which states:

"For the natural man receiveth not the things of the Spirit of God: for they are foolish unto him; neither can he know them; because they are spiritually discerned". (II Corinthians 2:14 KJV).

There is the key: God's truth is spiritually given; and, only to those individuals who are willing to receive that truth!

And yes, it is very helpful for one to draw upon the knowledge and efforts of those scholars who have made it their life's ambition to research God's Word; but you yourself can receive a tremendous blessing from God by getting to know Him through your personal study of the Scriptures. Regardless of what others might have led you to believe, God is a most loving and "Personal Being", as you will soon discover.

In bringing this book to you, I have done both: I have drawn upon the wisdom of scholars as well as fifty years of studying the Bible for myself.

Henry Ford is a very good example of a man who pursued life in this manner. His competitors took him to court claiming that he was not qualified to manufacture and sell automobiles because he did not have engineering degrees, designing degrees, marketing degrees, etc. When he was questioned by the court if this was true, he replied basically as follows:

'What man in my position does? I cannot be an expert in all these areas or my life would be spent becoming an expert, and no automobiles would get built. Therefore, I surround myself with, and employ the finest engineers, designers, and marketing people, and we work together to bring you the

> best automobiles that money can buy. And, the true test of
> what I claim is in the finished product'.

The truest test of what is being presented here is in the finished product. If you devote the time to read, "The Determining Factor", you will discover its worth. But please remember, you don't have to take my word for anything: just look around you and the truth will become self-evident: **as long as you know what things to look for** . . . thus, this book!

The Determining Factor is really an extension of an earlier book which I had written back in 1996, "Embrace the Truth, Prophesy Revealed through Current Events". This work was the accumulation of over thirty years of research. I'll admit, in some minor areas I was incorrect in my understanding; no one's perfect, right? However, probably 95% of what I wrote about has, indeed, unfolded just as it was presented; and it never ceases to amaze me how precise and accurate Biblical predictions are. And, as one studies these predictions over time, their fulfillment is all the more impressive.

I have made adjustments in those areas wherein I was mistaken, and have included updates where applicable. And, surprisingly, in recent research, I'm finding things unfolding faster than I am able to get the information into print; for I began this second work back in 2011 and Biblical predictions just keep on manifesting themselves right and left!

I'm not a writer and, in all honesty, have no desire to become one. However, I feel compelled to share what the Lord has placed upon my heart with all who are willing to listen. I have little to gain by publishing this work other than the satisfaction of knowing that I have obeyed the leading of God's Spirit, working within my own life. In all honesty, I have even utilized my own finances to put forth this book, because I am in total agreement with what Scripture says:

". . . The Lord is not slack concerning His promise, as some men count slackness, but is longsuffering to us-ward, not willing that any should perish, but that all should come to repentance". (II Peter 3:9 KJV).

There are a great many more prophetic wonders forthcoming, and it's imperative that mankind be prepared. However, most people are unaware of the warnings presented in the Bible concerning the last days. And, it is my hope, that through this work, you'll have at your disposal enough truth to enable you to make the changes necessary in your life, enabling you to experience the joy of Christ's saving grace, so that you might share in eternal glory with Him.

Don't ever let the time come when you must stand before your Creator and say: "Lord, I just didn't know or understand"; and then the Lord Almighty hands you a copy of this book and says: "I know you not, for I sent unto you my servant, Robert, to share the truth, and you would not listen"!

When I was a young grade-schooler I had difficulty understanding math. For some reason I couldn't comprehend why, when one multiplies two times two, they get four. This might sound ridiculous, but it was true. Finally, my dad said to me, "Bob, don't keep questioning why two times two equals four. Simply accept the fact that it does and math will make sense. And, behold, it worked!

When I quit struggling with the how and why, the rest became clear. That's the way one needs to look at the Scriptures. Quit doubting and simply begin believing and all else will become clear!

INTRODUCTION

ALTHOUGH THIS WORK BASICALLY concerns things pertaining to Biblical prophecies as they relate to the end of days in which we are living, the first chapter discusses money. Why money you may be asking? The love of money is the crux of every problem facing our civilization, and our current monetary system is about to collapse as foretold in Scripture (the Bible).

You see, whether one may realize it or not we're living under the heavy burden of a fraudulent **Fiat Money System** which will shortly bring down the entire economic structure of not only the United States of America, but every nation on the face of the globe. According to Webster's Dictionary, "Fiat Money" is money (currency) that is not convertible into coins or any specie of equivalent value"; it is money that is not backed by anything of value. As a result, money can, and is, being fraudulently manipulated by those having total control over the monetary system.

It is only fair to explain, however, that unless one totally and completely believes that all of Scripture is truly the unerring Word of God and that all arguments stating that the Bible is contradictory, and not trustworthy, because it was written by men (which, in part, is a misnomer), you will not be able to accept its truths and, therefore, benefit by them. One has a choice: he can believe in what man has to say, or in what God has to say . . . it can't be both ways.

In addition, one will find it difficult to accept why the end of things as we know them and why the soon return of Jesus Christ are close at hand. Hopefully, this work will erase all your doubts and provide you with the wisdom and understanding you're going to need in these last days as we know them.

Am I trying to scare you? To a degree, yes! But let me say that the governments of the world are doing a great job of that all by themselves. You don't need me to add to your burden. However, the message that I'm about to share with all who are willing to listen, is not only urgent, but it is imminent. If you put aside what is being shared within these pages and ignore the truth, you will be lost.

It would behoove the reader to consider what's being presented within these pages and to weigh each and every word very carefully. Please give yourself the opportunity to unlock Biblical truth; truth that may have escaped your understanding.

Jesus said in John 8:32 (KJV):

> "... If you continue in my word, then are ye my disciples indeed;
>
> And **ye shall know the truth,** and **the truth shall make you free**". (Bold print mine).

Focus in on the word "free" for it is the key. Just ask and it shall be given unto you.

We are all under the bondage of sin:

> "**If we say that we have no sin, we deceive ourselves, and the truth is not in us**". (1 John 1:8, KJV). (Bold print mine).

Many are under so great a bondage that they don't even recognize the state they are in, and that is very dangerous for one's soul.

Even Pontius Pilate had asked Jesus at His trial, "What is truth?" It is the answer to this vital question that can set free any individual and prepare that individual for the blessed return of Christ Jesus.

Jesus is the truth, for He stated so in John 14:6, (KJV):

> "I am the way, the truth and the life: no man cometh unto
> the Father, but by me".

Please notice that Jesus said that He was not only the truth, but also the way and the life. The way to eternal life is through Jesus; the truth are the Words He spoke while on this earth; and the life is what one will experience for all eternity when he or she accepts Christ Jesus.

The Bible, specifically from a prophetical view, can be compared to a jigsaw puzzle. Each individual piece (Scripture verse) holds limited meaning until sufficient verses are positioned into their proper places. When enough of the pieces (verses) are in their proper place, the picture will no longer be a puzzle, but truth which can be recognized and understood.

Dear Reader, the world is now at the point where enough of the pieces (or verses) of the prophetic puzzle are in their proper places, where anyone can visualize what's coming together if they will only look. In the Old Testament book of Daniel, the prophet, God commanded Daniel to write the following:

> "But thou, O Daniel, shut up the words, and seal the book,
> even to the time of the end: many shall run to and fro, and
> knowledge shall be increased". (Daniel 12:4, KJV).

Today we're living at a time when people travel globally (run to and fro), and where our knowledge has increased at an exponential rate.

We are at the point, because of our knowledge, that we can see not only the prophecies of the Bible unfolding before our very eyes, but we can conceive of how they actually can come about. This is brought to light in the chapter, "Great Mysteries Part III", which will be discussed at the end of this book.

Jesus said in Matthew 16:3 (KJV), when He was rebuking the Sadducees and Pharisees of His day (the Jewish Rabbis and religious teachers), that:

> "O ye hypocrites, ye can discern the face of the sky; but can
> ye not discern the signs of the times?"

The signs of the times that Jesus was referring to were Christ Jesus Himself and the miracles that He performed. Jesus gave up His divinity, became flesh and dwelt among men in order to teach men truth. Jesus performed hundreds of miracles, yet, most of the people (especially the Sadducees and Pharisees) did not discern that Jesus was God and that He was their longed for Messiah (or Savior). Jesus called them hypocrites because of their vain rejection of the truth.

Fast forward to 2016 and we find ourselves in the same boat. The signs are certainly all here. And I say to you, "Shall we too be hypocrites?" Or shall we . . . this time . . . open our minds and hearts and allow God's Truth to enter in that we should be saved.

This work, I pray, will enable you to do just that: Open Your Eyes and Heart!

In order to encourage you along your journey in understanding God's Holy Word, and in order to provide the impetus needed that you might look deeper into His Word, I'd like to share something I found quite interesting and, hopefully, you will also. It's all about "Laminins"!

"Laminins are a family of proteins that are an integral part of the structural scaffolding, of all base membranes, found in almost every type of animal tissue". Laminins are what holds us together, literally! They are called cell adhesion molecules because they hold one cell of our bodies to the next cell. Without them, everyone would literally fall apart. And, apparently, these cell adhesion molecules come together by sound (this concept will be explained at the end of this book).

Below is what the basic structure of a Laminin looks like. And, this is not a Christian portrayal of them either. Medical journals do depict them as such.

In Colossians 1:17 of the Amplified Bible, Paul states that:

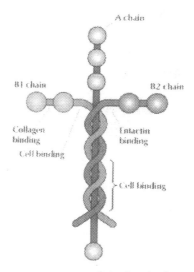

"And He Himself [Jesus Christ] existed before all things, and in Him [Jesus Christ] all things consist [cohere, are held together]". (Brackets mine).

What Paul is basically saying is that from a very literal standpoint, we are held together . . . one cell to another . . . by the cross! The cross of Christ Jesus is the glue that holds us together. And now, here in the 21th Century, we can peer into the very depths of our own amazing bodies and discover this truth hidden within each of us. In Romans 1:19-20 (KJV), Paul stated:

> ". . . that which may be known of God is manifest in them [men]: for God hath showed it unto them [men]. For the invisible things of him from the creation of the world are clearly seen, being understood by the things that are made, even his eternal power and Godhead; so that they are without excuse." (Brackets mine).

This is just one of many examples of how God has manifested Himself. There is an innate quality in each and every person that says there is a God, and that innate quality is clearly seen in our very own cellular makeup.

Read on now knowing that the Lord God is within you and that He will guide you to His truth . . . if you'll let Him.

CHAPTER ONE

THE FIAT MONEY SYSTEM

THE WORLD IS IN very serious trouble. There is no denying it. Man has allowed his so-called wisdom to replace the wisdom of Almighty God, and this is very dangerous, and has paved the way for an ever increasing evil presence to spread throughout the world. Man established a, "Fiat Money System", contrary to God's Biblical system as a means of exchange.

So what exactly is a "Fiat Money System"? It's a blatant system, designed to steal from the masses in order to make the rich wealthier, in an attempt to increase their power and control over our lives. This concept will become clearer after you read the chapter, "666 Prelude to Destruction". For now, let me provide some pertinent background.

I Timothy 6:10 (KJV) declares: "The love of money is the root of all evil". Mankind has replaced the principle of "honest money", which our forefathers wrote into the U.S. Constitution, and has replaced it with a dishonest weight and measure; which is our current "fiat paper money system". Please understand that the Bible doesn't proclaim money to be evil, just that the "love of money", is the root of all evil. Note also that this scripture states, "all evil", not just a portion of the evil that exists. What is being presented here is: **man's love of money is the basis for all his problems!**

This will become useless.

The result of man's greed, and need for power and control, has unleashed the economic crisis which began in October 2007 (and which is still with us), despite what our government might try and have us believe. And, its underlying potential to create a global economic collapse is inevitable.

So, what are willing to do? Shall we continue to lean on mankind's so-called wisdom to resolve our problems, or are we willing to finally turn to God's biblical principle of honest money? In order to trust in God, however, we must know exactly what the biblical principles of honest money are.

Most people, especially Americans, are misled to believe that our purpose in life is to obtain all the education we possibly can, get high paying jobs, accumulate all types of earthly possessions, and retire with life on easy street. Well, not to shock you my friends, that is not biblical. Let's take a look at what Matthew 6:26 (KJV) has to say:

> "Behold the fowls of the air: for they sow not, neither do they
> reap, nor gather into barns; yet your heavenly father feedeth
> them. Are ye not much better than they?"

Men dismiss the power behind such Scriptures because they refuse to accept the fact that God does, indeed, interact in our lives and in a very personal and intimate way. So why do men think this way? Because most men have the misguided notion that anything they accumulate is theirs. Men just can't seem to understand that the things they possess are actually gifts and blessings from Almighty God, and we are only stewards of those possessions. How do we know this is true? Well, God Himself proclaims that to be so. In the book of Haggai 2:8 (KJV), it states:

> "The silver is mine, and the gold is mine, says the Lord of hosts.

Also, in Psalms 50:10-12 (KJV), it clearly states:

> "For every beast of the field is Mine, and the cattle on a thousand hills. I know all the birds of the mountains, and the wild beasts of the field are Mine. If I were hungry, I would not tell you; for the world is Mine, and all its fullness".

Many individuals refuse to believe such Scripture because they do not want to give any credence to the fact that Scripture is the actual Word of God. Those that do believe, however, realize, without question, that everything does belong to the Lord and that the fullness of the world is truly His. Most believers can relate to how the Lord lovingly provides for them, and how the Lord gives them guidance through His Word, and how He expects us to steward His provisions. As a result, most believers are at peace with what's happening all around them, because they trust in the Lord and do not place their trust in fallible man. These individuals are preparing themselves for what's about to unfold, and it is my hope that you to will take heed as well.

Not being good stewards of what God has so freely provided to mankind is key to what's transpiring in the world today.

Mankind has not only distorted the concept of ownership, but the process of stewardship. God has provided us a tremendous example of who really owns the possessions we hold so dear to our lives, as shown in the biblical account of Job, where we read:

> "Then Job arose, and rent his mantle, and shaved his head, and fell down upon the ground, and worshiped. And said, naked I came out of my mother's womb, and naked shall I return thither: the Lord gave, and the Lord hath taken away; blessed be the name of the Lord". (Job 1:20-21, KJV).

Then in verse 22 it says:

> "In all this Job sinned not, nor charged God foolishly".

What a tremendous lesson to be learned here. Job lost everything: His family members, friends, cattle, sheep, oxen, goats, etc. Yet he realized that God owns everything, and we own nothing, and that God's will in our lives is the all-important issue. As a result of Job's "heart attitude" he did not place any blame on God . . . but, instead, worshipped Him. Because of his faithfulness to the Lord, the Lord not only replaced all that Job had lost, God actually increased Job's wealth.

Here is the point. This country was established on Christian principles, yet we have forsaken those principles, and the end result is that this country is falling apart. Also, as world leader, the effects of our foolishness have spread globally. As a Christian nation we have greater responsibility; but, we have failed miserably. Don't think for a moment that this lack of faithfulness on our part will go unpunished.

Having shared that, let me get into where the problem really lies and what we can do about it. Proverbs 22:7 (KJV), states:

"The rich ruleth over the poor, and the borrower is servant to the lender".

What does this mean? The answer: DEBT! We have become a debtor nation and are servants to those to whom we owe the debt. Conversely, the world is in total debt and, as a result, we are all servants to one another; and we are not servants in a good way, but in a negative way. It's a most vicious circle which was created intentionally by those few rich who have placed their allegiance in what the world has to offer, as well as mankind's wisdom, in lieu of God and His wisdom. The purpose, of course, is to control the masses and to ultimately have them serve the select few rich who have the power to do just that. This deterioration in men's rights and freedom is a result of our own ignorance and greed. The select few who are in control know that the best way to take advantage of our ignorance and greed is to control the money supply. What's that: Control our money supply? You bet! And, to accomplish that, those select few rich have had to create a system which would defile God's established principles, and replace those principles with their own. And what exactly did God establish as a standard for money? Gold and silver!

And why do you think that we have allowed this to happen to us? Mark 7:7-9, 13 (KJV), spells it out quite clearly:

> *"In vain do they worship me, teaching as doctrine the precepts of men. For letting go the commandment of God, you hold fast the traditions of men. Well do you nullify the commandment of God that you may keep your own tradition. You make void the commandment of God by your tradition".*

In short, Mark is simply saying that, <u>man has put aside God's ways in</u> <u>order to accommodate his own perceptions of how things should be.</u>

Our monetary system is no longer based on what God gave us and on that which our Constitution mandates; which is gold and silver. The current system is a false system; an illusion of something that we think is good but is, in actuality, quite evil. It's a "Fiat Money System" created only when the banking systems "lend" it into existence. Our current monetary system is debt based. What does this mean? It means that if our debt creation fails, our monetary system will soon collapse. And here's the real catcher: This country's debt is greater than its ability to pay off. Our country's debt is so astonishingly huge that we are, without doubt, at the point of no return . . . There's no getting around it!

Don't be fooled by the government or anyone else telling you otherwise. All you have to do is simply look around at everything that is now happening economically, and worldwide, and you'll discover that it's self-evident. In Genesis 2:10-12 (KJV), it states: *". . . and the gold of that land is good"*.

If God created gold and it was good, it had to be good for a reason. God created gold and silver as part of His provision for man. This is expressed in Genesis 13:2 (KJV):

> *"And Abram was very rich in livestock, in silver and in gold"*.

God provided Abram (the Lord changed his name to Abraham later in life) with much silver and gold. Gold was established as a store for value over the long term (savings), while silver was to be used as an ongoing source of money. Both were designed by God as an honest and true medium of exchange that would not allow men to use money to deceive others for their own selfish gain. It was God's form of money in order to benefit mankind.

In order for anything to be practical as a store for saving, however, it must maintain its value over time. Gold and silver do exactly that (as God had intended). You can fit all the refined gold in the world into a vault that measures eighteen meters (or approximately 58 feet) on each side.

Besides being an actual store of value and a practical means of exchange, there has to be an honest method of weight and measure. This is described in Leviticus 19:35 (KJV):

> "You shall do no injustice in judgment, in measurement of length, weight or volume".

Also, in Deuteronomy 25:15 (KJV), it says:

> "You shall have a perfect and just weight, a perfect and just measure, that your days may be lengthened in the land which the Lord your God is giving you."

Additionally, Proverbs 20:10 (KJV), states:

> "Diverse weights, and diverse measures, they are both alike, an abomination to the Lord".

In Hebrew, the word "diverse" means, "unjust" or "inconsistent". Apparently, God does consider an unjust and inconsistent weight and measure an abomination to Himself, and rightfully so. Who wouldn't be offended by someone providing an unjust and inconsistent basis on which things are figured?

However, today with the establishment of a "Fiat Money System", there is neither a just nor honest weight and measure involved in our system, and governments simply print paper money, at will, for whatever reason suits their needs and agendas.

I'm a collector of rare coins. When I was young I noticed that certain coins (like Reales or Pieces of Eight) had portions of their edges clipped off. I was always curious about this. As my knowledge grew, I learned the reason why. Governments and money changers would steal the peoples' money by cutting off the corners of coins, if you will, and taking the scraps from those clippings and melt them down to create even more coinage. This was accomplished with such subtlety that the masses would accept these clipped coins without even questioning why. By debasing or "clipping" the coins, the people were literally robbed of their money and this debasement of the coins was, in actuality, creating an unjust weight and measure; which was contrary to God's Word, as previously stated, but which I'll restate here for emphasis:

> "Diverse weights, and diverse measures, they are both alike, an abomination to the Lord".

Men think they are clever. Men have convinced themselves that since God is longsuffering and doesn't always execute judgment immediately that they can get away with evil. This is brought to light in Ecclesiastes 8:11 (KJV):

> "Because the sentence against an evil work is not executed speedily, therefore the heart of the sons of men is fully set in them to do evil".

The apostle Mark expressed this very thought in chapter 7:13-15 (KJV), of the book with his name:

> "Making the word of God of none effect through your tradition, which ye have delivered: and many such like things do ye.

Hearken unto me every one of you, and understand:

There is nothing from without a man, that entering into him can defile him: but the things which come out of him, those are they which defile him".

What Mark was saying here is that the thoughts of men's hearts are evil continually and men have replaced the precious Word of God by man's own tradition; therefore, making the laws of God of no effect. How true, and how sad!

What we have here is a form of monetary inflation. By clipping the coins the government and money changers (bankers) create inflation. Inflation is the government's way of stealing from the people because by melting down the scraps to create new as well as greater quantities of money, it devalues the coin's original worth. At the same time it places more money into the hands of government. Please take special note of what you're about to read for it is the method whereby our government and all governments steal from you and me:

Inflation is a planned and calculated method of robbing the people of their hard-earned money. Governments create inflation in order to fund their own inability to finance all their evil agendas legitimately. If governments kept to God's principles of using gold and silver as a standard for money they could not accomplish this. The many trillions of dollars that are being printed to continue funding the so-called stimulus programs (quantitative easing . . . a fancy term used to hide the real truth) is simply a scheme to enable the governments to pay down all their fraudulent and reckless spending. Printing money out of thin air certainly does devalue one's money. It's designed to eliminate the middle class, leaving only the poor and ultra rich. And the rich, of course, get richer, and the poor, well, they get poorer. Where have you heard that before?

Our government openly states that the recession of 2008-2009 is now over, and they also claim that inflation is not of major concern but, more likely, deflation. This is their insidious way to mislead an unsuspecting public. In addition, they do not include in their statistics such things as energy and food, and these things account for the major portion of one's living expenses.

Think carefully for a minute about what I'm about to share; because if you do think it through, you'll realize where things are headed.

> The government says that inflation is minimal and not to worry about it. Yet, I ask you, who hasn't felt the tremendous impact in gasoline prices, food prices, energy prices, etc. And these price increases are not small either. Regardless of what others might tell you, they're huge. For example, although gasoline prices escalate up and down on a regular basis, overall they're up over 100% since 2006. That's over 12% per year accumulative increases based on current 2015 prices (which, at this time, are only at their mid-point price in four years). Now, based on my own experience, food prices are up 35% in just the last two years and we not only buy less food, we don't purchase many of the costly items either. How about energy? Our electric costs are up 20% from three years ago and we run fewer electrical items than ever before.

So, let me ask you: "Who is kidding who?" It's all lies, deceptions, misleading tactics . . . it's all part of Satan's great master plan and he knows that if he can get men to displace God's principles with their own, he's won the battle.

Over the centuries all governments have debased money to such a great extent that ultimately their economies experienced a total collapse. And now, it's happening all over again; but this time it's worse, much worse; because the problem is global and not centered in just one country. If you were to research history you'd find that after every collapse, a return to God's principles of using gold and silver were re-established. Right now, most governments the world over are actively preparing themselves for financial collapse by hoarding gold and silver. It's in our daily news!

Interestingly, when one does search out economic collapses throughout history they'll also discover that **one inevitable fact presents itself: a moral collapse always occurred prior to an economic collapse.** And, not to anyone's great surprise, every nation on earth is in a moral collapse.

What we are experiencing today was brought to light in II Timothy 3:2 (KJV):

> *". . . For men will be lovers of themselves, lovers of money, boasters, proud, blasphemers, disobedient to parents, unthankful, unholy".*

Our forefathers would be in awe if they could see what has transpired in our beloved country and worldwide. To illustrate, let us take an in-depth look at our Constitution which was established by our Founding Fathers:

Article I, Section 10 states:

> *"No State shall enter into any Treaty, Alliance, or Confederation; grant Letters of Marque and Reprisal; coin Money, emit Bills of Credit; make anything but gold and silver Coin a Tender in Payment of Debt . . ."*

This article clearly states that nothing can be used but gold and silver coin as a tender of payment. So what happened?

Sadly, in Article I, Section 8, it states:

> "The Congress shall have power to lay and collect taxes, duties, imposts and excises, to pay debts and provide for the common defense and general welfare of the United States . . . to coin money, regulate the value thereof, and of foreign coin, and fix the standard of weights and measures".

Our Founding Fathers meant that the value of money is to be its precious metal content and that it's the precious metal content that gave any coin its real value.

The "Fiat Paper Money", that we hold so dear, has been made "status quo" via legal tender laws not in conformity with our beloved Constitution. Our Founding Fathers went to great lengths to avoid such a travesty. Our Founding Fathers made this quite clear for in Section 19 of the United States Coinage Act of 1792, we read:

> "SEC.19. And be it further enacted, That if any of the gold and silver coins which shall be struck or coined at the said Mint shall be debased or made worse as to the proportion of fine gold or fine silver therein contained, or shall be of less weight or value than the same ought to be pursuant to connivance of any of the officers or persons who shall be employed at the said Mint, for the purpose of profit or gain, officers or persons shall embezzle any of the metals which shall at any time be committed to their charge for the purpose of being coined at the said Mint, every such officer or person who shall commit any or either of the said offenses, shall be deemed guilty of felony, and shall suffer death".

WOW! I guess our Founding Fathers were quite serious about such criminal activity. Yet, the government and our elected officials accept and encourage such debauchery of our monetary system and they accomplish this via the Federal Reserve which, by the way, is not an agency of the Federal Government, but a privately owned and controlled institution set up by the select few rich. How is that possible? Dear reader, you tell me!

To further exasperate the situation, President Theodore Roosevelt, back in 1933, confiscated all gold and it no longer backs the dollar. Much more recently, silver was eliminated from our coinage.

How seriously was this debauchery taken? Let's consider what several of our most respected and talented personages have to say **(it's amazing!)**:

> "I sincerely believe . . . that the banking establishments are more dangerous than standing armies, and that the principle of spending money to be paid by posterity [our kids] under the name of funding is but swindling futurity [future generations] on a large scale". – Thomas Jefferson, 1816 (Brackets mine).

> "Whoever controls the volume of money in any country is absolute master of all industry and commerce". – James Garfield

> "The study of money, above all other fields in economics, is one in which complexity is used to disguise truth or evade truth, not reveal it". – John Kenneth Galbraith 1975.

> "Of all the contrivances for cheating the laboring classes of mankind, none has been more effective than that which deludes them with paper money". – Daniel Webster

"Money is the most important subject intellectual persons can investigate and reflect upon. It is so important that our present civilization may collapse unless it is widely understood and its defects remedied very soon". – Robert Hemphill, former credit manager, Federal Reserve Bank of Atlanta.

"All the perplexities, confusion and distress in America arise not from defects in the Constitution or confederation, nor from want of honor or virtue, as much as from downright ignorance of the nature of coin, credit and circulation". – John Adams

"Paper money has had the effect in your state that it will ever have, to ruin commerce, oppress the honest, and open the door to every species of fraud and injustice". – George Washington, in a 1787 letter to a Rhode Island legislator.

"With the exception only of the period of the gold standard, practically all governments of history have used their exclusive power to issue money to defraud and plunder the people". – Friedrich A. Hayek, Austrian economic and 1974 Nobel Prize-winner in economics.

What more needs to be said. Our government and the governments around the world are evil and their intentions are to confiscate the wealth of its citizens to advance their own evil agendas. More importantly, it's the select few rich who control the government. Satan is truly working deceptively in the minds and the hearts of all mankind; and, he has succeeded! And we, the people, are equally to blame. We have taken it upon ourselves to nullify the commandments of the Lord and have replaced them with our own traditions, exasperated by our ignorance and greed.

How have we the people done this? Most of the world has turned away from God because of our greed, selfishness, pride and arrogance. We have allowed evil to take hold of our leaders so that we can remain in our cozy comfort zones. We have allowed the world, the flesh and the devil to reign supreme in our lives and have pushed God out of our lives. How shameful we are!

Ever since the creation of the Federal Reserve in 1913, to when President Nixon had closed the gold window in the year 1971, God's principles have been uprooted and replaced by a "fiat money system". How much longer do you think it's going to take for our entire monetary system to collapse? Not much longer I can assure you.

We have gained more knowledge (not wisdom mind you) in the last fifty years than mankind has accumulated in the previous six thousand years. Things are happening in an exponential fashion. It is my firm belief that we have but a very few short years before our monetary system collapses (if not sooner; I'm being generous here folks). Even our current "fiat paper money system" is going to be replaced by a "moneyless system", as was prophesied in the Bible, and this "moneyless system" will, without any uncertainty, be under the singular control of none other than Antichrist himself. I'll prove this in upcoming chapters.

The following excerpt from an essay written by Mr. Alan Greenspan, former chairman of the Federal Reserve titled, "Gold and Economic Freedom", is included below for your consideration.

> *"In the absence of the gold standard, there is no way to protect savings from confiscation through inflation. There is no safe store of value. If there were, the government would have to make its holding illegal, as was done in the case of gold. If everyone decided, for example, to convert all his bank deposits to silver or copper or any other good, and*

thereafter decline to accept checks as payment for goods, bank deposits would lose their purchasing power and government-created bank credit would be worthless as a claim on goods. The financial policy of the welfare state requires that there be no way for the owners of wealth to protect themselves.

This is the shabby secret of the welfare statists' tirades against gold. Deficit spending is simply a scheme for the "hidden" confiscation of wealth. Gold stands in the way of this insidious process. It stands as a protector of property rights. If one grasps this, one has no difficulty in understanding the statists' antagonism toward the gold standard"

I placed this quote in bold italics for a very good reason. This is a statement by Alan Greenspan, former chairman of the Federal Reserve. I point to this quote in particular because it illustrates the audacity of one of our country's leaders and, our government above all, to blatantly say, in effect, that, "You people of the United States of America are ignorant and very foolish. Here we are, able to publically confess our sin to place into captivity the masses in order that we might gain wealth and power at your expense and there is nothing you can do about it".

Read it again and again, my friends; and read it carefully. If you're not totally convinced by Mr. Greenspan's statement that there is an agenda in place that is so evil, that it has to be Satanic in origin, then there is no more for me to say. But if you can see through all the lies, deception and conniving and wish to understand more with the hope of saving yourself, your family, and friends from ultimate disaster, then please read though this entire book as often as is necessary for things to kick in and make sense. The Lord forbid that you don't!

Before closing this chapter I would like to express the views of world renowned economist, Ludwig Von Mises:

> *"There is no means of avoiding the final collapse of a boom brought about by credit expansion. The alternative is only whether the crisis should come sooner as the result of voluntary abandonment of further credit expansion, or later as a final and total collapse of the currency system involved".*

Dear reader, the collapse will come, and sooner than later! How do I know? For three reasons:

1.) The Bible states that this will be so.

2.) Our governments have chosen not to go the route of voluntarily abandoning further credit expansion, and

3.) We are now beyond the point of no return and a moneyless system is the only way out. And, that system, has already been set in motion as you'll soon discover. I'll be explaining about this in the chapter titled, "666, Prelude to Destruction".

This might be frightening to hear, but be of good cheer, for there is a way out:

Turn to Christ Jesus for He is faithful and loving and will keep you safe from the trials to come; and they will come. In Hebrew, the name for Jesus is "JESHUA", which means safety. Only in Jesus Christ is there safety. In the chapters to come, you'll soon discover why!

So please don't set this book aside and forget it. This book is your hope beyond hope. Just keep on reading and you'll discover why this is so.

CHAPTER TWO
"666" PRELUDE TO DESTRUCTION

IF YOU RECALL, IN the book of Daniel the prophet, chapter 12:4, the angel of the Lord told Daniel to:

> "... shut up the words, and seal the book, even to the time
> of the end: many shall run to and fro, and knowledge shall
> be increased".

What is being stated here is that when men have gained sufficient knowledge enabling them to understand certain prophetic Scriptures, the time would be ripe for the return of Christ Jesus and the setting up of His kingdom on earth.

Never has knowledge increased so exponentially than it has during this past century. We can certainly relate to more concepts than ever before. We understand airplanes, space travel, galaxies, and dematerialization/rematerialization of matter, black holes, and so much more. Back in Daniel's time he had no idea of what an airplane was, for example. Daniel would most likely have had a difficult time describing a plane even if he had experienced one. However, because of our vast knowledge, we can conceptualize just about anything.

Let's see if we can conceptualize the following: In Brussels, headquarters of the European Union, an exceptionally large computer system exists taking up more than three stories of the administration building. According to Dr. Hendrick Elderman, a former chief analyst of the Common Market, now known as the European Union (EU), this gigantic computer was designed to assign each and every person in the world a number (mark) to be used in all buying and selling transactions. The idea is that by creating a digital units system employing the number "666" (see the illustration below) every individual on the face of the planet earth could be assigned a number, or digital mark and, without which, a person could not buy or sell, hold a job, collect social security, drive a car, etc. They also concluded that this number or mark would best be affixed on a person's forehead or on the back of their hand.

Note the three sets of double lines at the beginning, middle and end of the bar code.

The actual number "666" does not appear on UPC labels. These three sets of fine double lines that appear at the beginning, middle and at the end of the UPC code are read by the scanner as "666". Our leaders intentionally suppressed the number "666" due to the general publics' awareness of the Biblical implications behind such a number. This is just another devious method by our governments to deceive the masses.

Some of you might feel that this is ridiculous. No one would ever agree to a number or mark being affixed to their forehead or the back of their hand. That would be comparable to what Hitler did to the Jews during the second World War, and no one would tolerate such an indignity again. However, tattooing on one's body is very commonplace these days and many do not even give such markings a second thought. In fact, those that do have such markings do so because they actually enjoy having them and many find meaning and expression by employing such markings. Having shared this, however, there is a way to mark one's body without visible signs for those who might find the idea objectionable.

As recently as 1975, an effective method of invisibly tattooing fish, poultry and meat was invented. This system, called "laser tattooing", is totally invisible and can be affixed to human flesh in a matter of seconds and with virtually no pain experienced by the recipient.

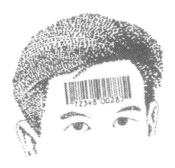

This laser-tattooed number or mark would only be visible to infrared scanners which are placed at every checkout counter and place of business (as well as government institutions). It would enable the world to do away with all currency, coins, and credit cards.

Many people are unaware that such a system as this already exists but one can easily verify this by simply checking UPC Bar Code labels on products in one's own kitchen pantry. Please take note, however, that when doing so, you might find some items don't appear to have the three sets of double lines running down the beginning, the middle, and end of the bar code label. The reasoning for that is, some items might have come in bulk containers and only the bulk containers would have the three sets of double lines and any items contained therein would employ a slightly different style of bar code labeling as a result. Most all common household goods, for example, would show the three sets of double lines.

Astonishingly, as of January 1995, all UPC code labels, used on products for purchase or sale, are now encoded with this "666": that's 100%; not some, but all.

UPC code labels used to identify any materials not designated for purchase/resale transactions, such as raw materials, would not be required to have "666" coding as just described. Such products are encoded slightly differently, but they still do contain the "666" somewhere along the processing line.

This is quite interesting seeing as how the Bible states that, the number or mark, would only be required **"For buying and for selling"** purposes; for we read in Revelation 13:15-18 (KJV):

> "And he [Antichrist] causeth all, both small and great, rich and poor, free and bond, to receive a mark in their right hand, or in their foreheads: and **that no man may buy or sell,** save he that had the mark, **or the number** of the beast, or the number of his [Antichrist's] name. Here is wisdom. Let him that hath understanding count the number of the beast: for it is the number of a man, and his number is six hundred threescore and six [666]". (Brackets and bold print mine).

Why do you think that the Bible indicates that it would take understanding . . . six, six, six seems simple enough. However, it goes far, far beyond a simple numerical designation for a man. Again, Revelation 13:18 (KJV) says:

"Let him that hath understanding count the number of the beast [Antichrist]". (Brackets mine).

Counting certainly infers a deciphering process. Therefore, "666" represents a code within itself. Even a most simplified bar code style arrangement contains a great deal more hidden information. The numbers printed beneath the various bars, when scanned, go through four separate reading processes. Also, the numeric equivalent bars on the left side of any UPC label are the opposite of those located on the right side of the label. This is designed to help separate information contained therein while at the very same time it allows more information to be stored. All viable information about a person could be hidden within a bar code.

The purpose behind this numbering system (so the world governments want us to believe), is to address such problems as lost or stolen credit cards and money; reduce crime (without money and credit cards there would be less incentive for criminals to steal); to limit the effects of inflation (when governments can't print money it reduces inflation); curb all credit spending and, therefore, reduce all debts, (for if you do not have sufficient credits stored in the central computer system of banks, it will be impossible for anyone to complete a transaction). In short, your entire life-style will be dictated by a numbering system, which, in turn, will be controlled by central computers; and those will eventually be under Antichrist's control.

INTERESTING THOUGHT

It's public knowledge that the United States of America has been endeavoring to establish a "National ID" system and has made many attempts to do so. Thank the Lord, at least for now anyway, that many states are fighting this concept. Why? Well, believe it or not, these states feel that a "National ID" system would lead up to the "666" numbering system revealed in Scripture. Now that's something to munch on"!

In an article noted in Moody Monthly, back in March of 1974, one of the European Union leaders was asked:

> *"What would the Confederacy do if a person refused to cooperate with this system?"*

The leader's answer was:

> *". . . We would use force to make him cooperate".*

How very nice of one of our world leaders to be so expressive concerning government's intentions for its citizens. Thanks guys, we love you too!

It is my firm belief that in today's technologically advanced societies, rather than employing laser tattooing only on a person's forehead, or on the back of their hand, that a new device, such as the "Digital Angel", will most likely be implemented. "Digital Angel" is a "microchip" device currently used to track people's pets and, although it's small in size, perhaps the size of a large grain of rice, it would leave a slight bump when implanted in an individual's forehead. Personally, I'm of the belief that, when Antichrist takes control, and forces people to take his number and/or mark, that the UPC Bar Code, using laser-tattooing techniques will be employed to mark one's forehead, while the "Digital Angel" device will be implanted in the back of one's hand.

One might find it difficult to believe that this is happening today, so allow me to provide you with an article dated November 1, 2000 from, WorldNetDaily.com:

"A NASDAQ –traded company has finally unveiled its long-touted and most highly controversial "Digital Angel" – a sub-dermal microchip implant designed not merely for keeping tabs on pets, but for widespread, worldwide use in tracking human beings".

OUCH! What a sneaky way for keeping tabs on human beings that are considered to be "anti-government". And, yes, there are some very good uses for such a device, as in the healthcare arena. However, like all great inventions, the government reins in and uses them for their evil agendas.

What's also very interesting is how easily this device can be affixed (inserted) into people. The article goes on to say:

". . . The technology consists of a miniature sensor device, designed to be implanted just under the skin".

There you go! How about implanting this device under the skin on your right hand; then tell me that John (the writer of Revelation), didn't know what he was talking about. Just maybe, he didn't: many of the prophets had no understanding of the prophecies that they were commanded of God to write. They just wrote down what God instructed them to write (you know, the Inspired Word of God which people find difficult to accept).

This same WorldNetDaily.com article also had an interview with the chief scientist, Dr. Peter Zhou, where they stated:

". . . he believes the implant will be as popular as cell phones and vaccines".

GOSH! It appears that most individuals will find this type of "device-implanting" to be a great way to improve their lives. Just think about it: there wouldn't be any credit cards to contend with, no bothering with money, a fantastic method to keep medical records safe and readily available, to help find missing children, adults and pets . . . what more could one ask?

The unsuspecting masses are going to grab this up eagerly . . . **But Wait!** What does the Bible have to say about those who elect to accept this numbering system: allowing it to be tattooed on their forehead or implanted on one's hand? Revelation 14:9-10 (KJV) spells it out quite succinctly:

> "And the third angel followed them, saying with a loud voice, if any man worship the beast [Antichrist] or his image, and receive his mark in his forehead, or in his hand, the same shall drink of the wine of the wrath of God, which is poured out without mixture into the cup of his indignation; And he shall be tormented with fire and brimstone in the presence of the Holy Angels, and in the presence of the Lamb [Christ Jesus]: And they shall have no rest day or night, who worship the beast and his image, and whosoever receiveth the mark of his [Antichrist's] name". (Brackets mine).

This is scary stuff, right? Well, that might be so for those who refuse to place their trust in Jesus Christ as their Lord and Savior; but not for those who do believe. You see, for anyone who believes, they will escape those things that are about to come upon the earth in the near future. Why? Because that is what the Lord promised to those that do trust in Him.

Please consider the following: You might be thinking to yourself, "I can't possibly believe in all this . . . it's all a bunch of malarkey". Well, tell me how John, the apostle, was able to write about these things back almost two thousand years ago? And, if you're thinking to yourself, "I don't believe that a man by the name of John wrote about such things back then, for there isn't any proof"; then how do you explain how back in 1611 (more than four hundred years ago) when the first Bible was translated into English, that all these things were prophesied by John and then written down. They had to come from somewhere. And, if they're as old as 1611 (for we have the original 1611 version in archives) how did anyone know even that far back that any such things would come into being unless God inspired someone like John to put these things into written form? Obviously, the writing is on the wall . . . all one has to do is see and believe!

We're living at a time when so much of God's Word is being fulfilled that it's like people can't see the forest because of the trees. God forbid that any of us should open our hearts and our minds, letting the truth set us free from all our sins.

Here's the greatest lie of all according to this same article, for Dr. Zhou states:

> "Digital Angel will be a connection from yourself to the electronic world . . . **It will be your guardian, protector** . . . **It will bring good things to you** . . . **We'll be a hybrid of electronic intelligence and our own soul**". (Emphasis mine).

I don't want to be a hybrid of anything! I don't need the protection of "Digital Angel", for I have God's protection, and only God can provide any "good thing".

Oh, by the way, the Food and Drug Administration already approved this device for implantation into humans back in 2004.

In the near future if you haven't already been removed from the earth in an event called the "Rapture", you will, without doubt, be called upon to take Antichrist's number and/or mark on the forehead and back of your hand. **DO NOT DO IT**! If you do, you'll be utterly damned forever. This is not some fictional episode out of "Buck Rogers in the 21ˢᵗ Century". This is very real, very near and very dangerous.

At this juncture I would like to clarify a point for those who decide to get out their Bible and read Revelation 13:11-18 (KJV). Mention is made of two beasts and this might prove to be confusing for some. However, it is easily explained. The first beast is actually the Antichrist. The second beast is someone referred to as the "False Prophet". The first beast, Antichrist, is a man who is a political leader. The second beast, the False Prophet, is someone who will be a religious leader.

God is making known to mankind that in the "End Times", two men will come into being: one will capture the hearts of the secular world; the other will capture the hearts of the religious minded of the world. The Antichrist and the False Prophet will both be given great power and authority by Satan himself. However, it is Antichrist who will receive the highest honor, while the False Prophet will inspire people to worship Antichrist and to accept his number and/ or mark (or both).

This moneyless system will already be in force when Antichrist dominates during the Tribulation Period (I'll be explaining about this period in the next chapter) and will be supported by the False Prophet. People will be caught unaware and this system of control will strike mankind full force throughout most of the earth; mainly, though, in the European countries. Before people understand what is happening to them, they will be confronted with a choice: Take the number and/or mark and exist, or refuse the number and/or mark, and pay the penalty for not conforming. And, as previously noted, one of the European Union leaders stated that if people don't conform to the system, government will use force to make them conform.

Once Antichrist does make his debut, then will the Tribulation begin. This period will last for seven years and will constitute the last seven years on earth under mankind's rule. At the end of the seven years of tribulation the greatest battle ever to be waged on earth will occur . . . "The Battle of Armageddon"! I will expound on this extremely important period in human history in chapter three, "Tribulation & Armageddon".

For now let's read what Paul Henry Spaak, past Secretary General of NATO once remarked:

> *"We need no new commissions, we have too many already. What we need is a man who is great enough to keep all people in subjection to him and to lift us out of the economic bog in which we threaten to sink. Send us such a man. Be he a god or a devil: we will accept him".*

I've placed this quotation in bold italics in order to emphasize the gravity of what's going on in the world today and the insidious measures that mankind is willing to take in order to resolve all these problems. There is hope, however; but only in Christ Jesus will this hope come. Rest assured in that.

Henry Spaak's statement: "Be he a god or devil, we will accept him", is quite disconcerting to say the least. Antichrist will be the person who people will appoint to accept the challenge. However, he will not be a god or a devil, but a man (Revelation 13:18); a man endued with great power by Satan; and he will set himself up to be a god as foretold in Daniel 11:36 (KJV).

Please also note what Paul Henry Spaak states is the primary problem . . . **an economic bog!** That's expressing it mildly.

Today, for the first time in the history of mankind, has this concept of **an economic bog** manifested itself throughout the entire globe, starting in 2007. And regardless of what others are telling you, this recession is far from being over. It will escalate into unbelievable proportions over the next few years (if not sooner).

We're at the beginning of a worldwide monetary collapse, and everything is in place for this "moneyless system" to take root, enabling Antichrist to make his debut. It isn't stated in the Bible exactly how long it will be after the monetary collapse occurs that Antichrist will show his ugly face: However, it is speculated that it can't be too very long because a worldwide monetary collapse would create such devastation that all of mankind would be looking for someone to come along, and quickly, who is able to resolve these problems. Just a thought!

Matthew 13:10-17 (KJV) clearly stipulates why mankind is on the brink of destruction:

> "This people's heart is waxed gross, and their ears are dull
> of hearing, and their eyes they have closed; lest at any time
> they should see with their eyes and hear with their ears,
> and should understand with their hearts, and should be
> converted, and I should heal them".

Truly we have allowed our hearts to wax gross and have allowed our ears to become dull of hearing; and our eyes blinded to seeing the truth; and our hearts rejecting understanding. May the Lord our God forgive us all!

We are certainly a spoiled nation. We have allowed ourselves to lose sight of what is most important. Haggai 1:5-6 (KJV) declares:

> "Consider your ways. Ye have sown much, and bring in little; ye eat, but ye have not enough; ye drink, but ye are not filled with drink; ye clothe you, but there is none warm; and he that earneth wages earneth wages to put into a bag with holes".

In Revelation 3:15-17 (KJV) Jesus rebukes the end-time church of Laodicea (a representation of the church of the end times in which we now live) with these words:

> "I know thy works, that thou art neither cold nor hot: I would thou wert cold or hot. So then because thou art lukewarm, and neither cold nor hot, I will spue thee out of my mouth. Because thou sayest, I am rich, and increased with goods, and have need of nothing; and knoweth not that thou art wretched, and miserable, and poor, and blind, and naked".

Many Christians today are becoming apathetic and indifferent and refuse to take a sound stand in their Christian walk. How can they, for they don't spend sufficient time (if any time at all) in God's Word (the Bible). Their hearts are not God-centered but, rather, self-centered.

Please keep the following thought in mind. Jesus said in Matthew 20:16 (KJV):

> ". . . for many are called, but few are chosen".

One needs to believe from his/her heart and not just a passive intellectual belief. One must also put his/her belief to work.

In Galatians 6:7-8 (KJV) it states:

> "Be not deceived: God is not mocked: for whatever a man soweth, that shall he reap. For he that soweth to the flesh shall of the flesh reap corruption; but he that soweth to the Spirit shall of the spirit reap life everlasting".

Please consider giving your life to Christ Jesus!

CHAPTER THREE

TRIBULATION & ARMAGEDDON

BEFORE DISCUSSING THE EVENTS of the Tribulation and Armageddon, it's imperative that I emphasize that, without adequate background in Scripture, it would be most difficult for the layman to try and comprehend Daniel's prophesy concerning this time period. Therefore, as briefly as I can, I will supply the reader with an interpretation of the main points only. If you do wish a more detailed breakdown I suggest that you secure a copy of Dr. Alva J. McClain's book entitled, "Daniel's Prophesy of the Seventy Weeks", by Zondervan. Portions of what I am presenting here are concepts as noted in Dr. McClain's book, which I will use as a guide should you decide to expand your horizons on this topic.

Let's begin with the prophecy itself, as found in Daniel 9:24-27(KJV), and then we can break down all of its components:

> VERSE 24: "Seventy weeks are determined upon thy people and upon thy Holy City, to finish the transgression, and to make an end of sins, and to make reconciliation for iniquity, and to bring in everlasting righteousness, and to seal up the vision and prophesy, and to anoint the Most Holy."

> VERSE 25: "Know therefore, and understand, that from the going forth of the commandment to restore and to build Jerusalem unto Messiah the Prince shall be seven weeks,

and threescore and two weeks: the street shall be built again, and the wall, even in troublesome times".

VERSE 26: "And after threescore and two weeks shall Messiah be cut off, but not for himself: and the people of the prince to come that shall destroy the city and the sanctuary; and the end thereof shall be with a flood, and unto the end of the war desolations are determined".

VERSE 27: "And he shall confirm the covenant with many for one week; and in the midst of the week he shall cause the sacrifice and the oblation to cease, and for the overspreading of abominations he shall make it desolate, even until the consummation, and that determined shall be poured upon the desolate".

This prophesy might seem somewhat confusing at first but it should become much clearer to you as we break down what Daniel predicted.

A.) This entire prophesy concerns Israel and the city of Jerusalem.
B.) Two different princes are mentioned . . . "Messiah the Prince" (verse 25), and the "Prince that shall come" (verse 26).
C.) The total time span of the prophecy is 70 weeks and these weeks are broken down into lesser weeks . . . 1.) Seven weeks; 2.) Threescore and two weeks and, 3.) One week.
D.) The beginning of the 70 weeks started with: "The going forth of the Lord's commandment to restore and to build Jerusalem".
E.) The end of 7 weeks, and the threescore and two weeks will be notably marked by the appearance of "Messiah the Prince" of Israel (Jesus Christ).

F.) After the threescore and two weeks time, "Messiah the Prince", Christ, is cut off (crucified), and Jerusalem again will be destroyed.

G.) The seventieth week, or last week, will be revealed by the establishment of a firm covenant (or treaty) between the coming prince (Antichrist) and Israel.

H.) In the middle of this last (final) week, the coming prince breaks his covenant with the Jewish nation of Israel and forbids the worship in the Jewish Temple . . . all "oblations and sacrifices" will be terminated.

That's quite a bit for one to chew on without some further explanation, so please allow me to provide some background for you.

It should be understood that the weeks referred to in this prophesy are considered weeks of years and not weeks of days (refer to chapter six, entitled, "Mathematics in Scripture", for an explanation about weeks in the Bible). In other words, the seventy weeks are actually 490 years in total: The length of these prophetic years is 360 days (based on the Hebrew calendar).

This entire period of weeks first began with the commandment to rebuild Jerusalem . . . for Jerusalem had been destroyed back in 586BC by the Babylonians. This was accomplished by the decree issued by King Artaxerxes on March 14, 445BC (please refer to Nehemiah 2:1-8 in the Old Testament). Now, from March 14, 445BC, to the appearance of Jesus Christ, "Messiah the Prince", was exactly 69 weeks (of years) or, 483 years in total (69 weeks times 7 years = 483 years). At the end of these 69 weeks of years, to the very day, April 6, 32AD, Jesus Christ rode up to Jerusalem on the "foal of an ass" (donkey), in fulfillment of the well-known prediction of Zechariah 9:9 (KJV) which states:

> "Rejoice greatly, O Daughter of Zion; shout, O Daughter of
> Jerusalem: Behold, thy King cometh unto thee: he is just,
> and having salvation; lowly, and riding upon an ass, and
> upon the foal of an ass".

With this portion of the prophecy having been fulfilled we can appreciate how chronologically accurate Daniel's prophecy really was up to and including the 69th week, or first 483 years.

In analyzing the last week of the prophecy (or last seven year period), you will need to understand a most important fact: the entire period of the "70 weeks prophecy" does not follow consecutively; only the first 69 weeks. The last week will not occur until sometime in the near future. This GAP in time between the 69th and 70th week is termed, "Prophetic Parenthesis", by Bible Scholars.

It is a well known fact that prophets, when given visions, report only what they see in the vision and nothing more. The prophets can see many things throughout history and pen them down all in one prophetic statement. Only details within the prediction will allow one to separate gaps in time. Bible scholars know exactly what to look for in any prophecy which might call for a "time gap", or Prophetic Parenthesis, to be considered.

Even movie producers use such a technique in their films to create effect and clarification, as well as impact.

What's important to understand is that many of the prophecies, to which accurate interpretations could not be determined until mankind gained in knowledge of things unknown during Daniel's day, have now been unveiled. This is very clear, for in Daniel 12:4 (KJV), as previously noted, it says:

"But thou, O Daniel, shut up the words, and seal the book, even to the time of the end: many shall run to and fro, and knowledge shall be increased".

The last week of Daniel's prophecy is yet in the future. However, it is not as far into the future as some think. According to the Bible, this last week will be ushered in when four main events take place:

1.) Israel becomes a nation once again. This occurred back in 1948 when the Balfour Declaration was issued by Great Britain.
2.) When an empire comes into existence, consisting of ten nations (kingdoms), and encompassing a major portion of the Old Roman Empire. This specific empire will be discussed in the chapter titled, "The Last World Empire".
3.) A numbering system employing the "666" concept is established and,
4.) Antichrist makes his debut.

"One", above, has taken place. When Great Britain issued the Balfour Declaration back in 1948, it allowed the Jews to repossess their promised land in Jerusalem.

"Two" and "three" are currently in the process of being fulfilled. We have already discussed item "three", the "666" numbering system in chapter two. As for item "two", the end-time empire, it will be addressed in chapter five, "The Last World Empire". The Last World Empire is none other than the European Union.

Things are developing rapidly even as this book is being written.

"Four" is yet future; but Antichrist's appearance is very close at hand. There is little doubt in my mind that Antichrist is alive and well on planet earth as we speak.

Once Antichrist makes his debut, the last seven years of Daniel's prophecy will commence. This last seven years is well known as the Tribulation Period, (it is also referred to in the Scriptures as the, "Time of Jacob's Trouble"). This seven year period will be filled with much pain and suffering, turmoil, wars and rumors of wars, disease, and both natural and supernatural happenings. This time period has been portrayed in many books, movies and TV specials, such as: the "Left Behind" series, the "Discovery Channel", the "History Channel" and others. It will be a time when, not only natural catastrophes will dominate, but supernatural events. During the first half of the Tribulation, the unfortunate individuals who were not removed from the earth in an event called the, "Rapture", will experience a great deal of suffering and religious persecution. During the second half of the Tribulation Period, or last 3-1/2 years, also referred to as the <u>Great</u> Tribulation, not only will those left behind experience religious persecution, natural catastrophes, disease, etc., but the wrath of Satan will come upon mankind in supernatural ways. In addition, God will manifest His wrath by withdrawing His providential hand upon mankind and allowing Satan to have his way.

The terrifying events to befall mankind during the Tribulation are to be found throughout Revelation 5 through Revelation 20. These chapters discuss, for example . . . the Four Horsemen of the Apocalypse, the Seven Seal Judgments, the Seven Trumpet Judgments, and lastly, the Seven Vial Judgments (all of which have been made into TV specials). I won't take the time to discuss these events for lack of space and for the fact that one can rent videos pertaining to these things.

As stated, the Tribulation begins with the debut of Antichrist and with his confirming the seven year covenant as was previously mentioned. Antichrist will not be the one to construct this covenant; for it will have already been written; and is, in fact, in the hands of our Secretary of State, John Kerry, (it only requires a bit more polishing, if you will). Antichrist will only confirm this covenant with Israel and will promise to protect Israel from her many enemies. In the middle of the tribulation, Antichrist will break the Treaty and turn against Israel. Antichrist will also commit the sin of sins by entering into the new Jewish Temple on Mt. Mariah (which Temple is still to be built, but is in the final drawing stages). When Antichrist enters into the Jewish Temple, he does so to proclaim himself as the god of this world. The Scriptures call this: "The Abomination of Desolation". At this happening, all hell will literally break lose, for we read in Matthew 24:15 & 21 (KJV):

> "When ye shall see the abomination of desolation, spoken of by Daniel the prophet, stand in the holy place, (whoso readeth, let him understand). . ."

> "For then shall be great tribulation, such as was not since the beginning of the world to this time, nor shall there ever be".

Immediately upon his breaking the covenant, the Antichrist will enforce the moneyless system and the "666" numbering initiative, in an attempt to take control of most of the world's commerce, and industry, and especially, the population of earth.

During the Tribulation Period many things will happen: both natural, as well as supernatural, as previously explained. It will be a period of both peace and turmoil: but only a temporary peace, for the world will adhere to Antichrist's dictatorship. However, once Antichrist breaks the covenant with Israel, the turmoil will escalate to unbelievable proportions.

Antichrist comes on the scene when there is worldwide economic, social, and political unrest (sounds like what's transpiring right now, no?). It will begin at a time when people everywhere will be crying loudly for ONE PERSON to solve their woes.

Remember the quote I presented by Paul Henry Spaak? He said that: "What is needed is a man who can put all people in subjection to him, and whether he be a god or devil, we'll accept him". Well, Antichrist will be that man.

While Israel is experiencing a much sought after peace, and while many nations will be enjoying increased economic stability, reduced inflation, and temporary ceasing of conflicts between certain countries that will be at war; the Christians will be going through many trials. These are only the Christians who didn't accept Christ Jesus as their Lord and Savior prior to the "Rapture" having taken place, and the onset of the Tribulation; but who, having finally realized their mistake, will have turned their lives over to the Lord during the Tribulation. These new Christians will most likely have to endure many trials until the Lord takes them home. Also, during this period, newly born Christians will be unable to buy or sell, hold jobs, drive cars, obtain food, etc., because they'll have refused to take the number and/or the mark of Antichrist and will not give obeisance to him. In the beginning, these Christians will be punished by imprisonment. Most likely, during the last half of the Tribulation many, but not all, remaining Christians, will be put to death.

The death penalty during the Tribulation will be the act of beheading according to the Bible; for in Revelation 20:4 (KJV) it states:

> "And I (John) saw thrones, and they that sat upon them, and judgment was given unto them: And I saw the souls of them that were beheaded for the witness of Jesus, and for the Word of God, and which had not received his mark

upon their foreheads or in their hands; and they lived and
reigned with Christ a thousand years".

The current form of execution by the Islamic State is by means of beheading? This form of execution will become the norm. How could John know this unless he was inspired by God?

The purpose of the Tribulation is six-fold:

1.) "To finish the transgression" (to put a stop to Israel's rebellion against God),
2.) "To make an end of sins",
3.) "To make reconciliation for iniquity",
4.) "To bring in everlasting righteousness",
5.) "To seal up the vision [which Daniel was given] and the prophecy, and
6.) "To anoint the Most Holy".

Actually, there is another reason why God will allow this persecution to take place. If men won't accept Jesus Christ as their Lord and Savior while there is still a modicum of peace left on the earth, then perhaps, if mankind is forced to experience great tribulation, they might finally come back to God. Most, however, will not, but many will; and God is anxious to save as many as can be saved before His plan for mankind is fulfilled.

Christ Jesus will soon return to finalize all of the above. He desires that all mankind should turn to Him before He comes back as so shown in II Peter 3:9 (KJV), where he shares Christ's desire:

> *"The Lord is not slack concerning His promise, as some*
> *men count slackness, but is longsuffering toward us, not*
> *willing that any should perish but that all should come to*
> *repentance".*

Since most of the world has rejected Jesus Christ as their Lord and Savor, and since the world has chosen to go the way of Satan, God will withhold His providential hand during the Tribulation and allow Satan to bring forth untold destruction and misery upon all of mankind. Without God's direct supernatural intervention, there would not be any flesh left alive, as is so stated in Scripture.

In the final analysis, everything will end with the greatest battle the world will ever experience . . . the "Battle of Armageddon".

Armageddon **will not be fought** between two sets of earthly nations. It will be a battle between the armies of heaven, under Christ and His saints, and the armies of the earth, under Satan, the Antichrist, and the False Prophet; as well as the nations that have pledged allegiance to Antichrist.

On Christ's side there will be Israel (Zech. 14:1-15), the angels of God (Matt. 25:31-45, II Thess. 1:7-10), and the resurrected saints throughout all the ages (Zech. 14:1-5, Jude 14, Rev. 19:11-21).

On Antichrist's side there will be the devil (Satan) along with his fallen angels and demons (Rev. 12:7-12, 16:13-16, and Rev. 20:1-3), the ten kings heading up the ten nations of the last world empire, (Rev. 17:14-17, Dan. 2:44; 7:19-27), the countries north and east of the ten kingdoms (Dan. 11:44, Ezek. 38,39, Rev. 16:12), and other nations who will co-operate with the Antichrist (Rev. 16:13-16, Zech. 14:1-5, 16, Ezek. 38, 39).

Due to lack of space, I haven't written out the Scripture verses pertaining to those who will be participating in the Battle of Armageddon (as I have throughout this work) because there are simply too many. Having said that, however, I would highly recommend that you look up the above verses and study them carefully, for they are interesting.

The purpose of God will be to deliver Israel from complete destruction by the hands of Antichrist and all the nations who want to annihilate the Jewish people (Zech. 14, Isa. 63:1-10); to punish all these nations for persecuting the Jews (Matt. 25:31-46); to set up a kingdom on the earth with Christ Jesus as its head (Dan. 7:13, 14, Luke 1:32); to rid the earth of all rebellion and to restore God's dominion on earth as before the fall of Adam and Eve (I Corth. 15:24-29, Eph. 1:10); to allow man one more dispensational test (this will be the Millennium or 1,000 year rule of Christ on earth) before destroying every rebel on the planet (Rev. 21:1-22, and Rev. 5, II Pet. 3:10-13).

The purpose of Antichrist, Satan and man will be to stop God's plan for taking over all the earthly governments, and to avert their own impending doom (Rev.12:12, 19:19-21, 20:1-10, Zech.14:1-5).

Just think of the power and majesty of Jesus Christ to be capable of defeating the armies of earth, which will be 200 million men strong, and to do so in a single day (as Revelation describes).

There is no escaping what's coming down the pike except one receives Jesus Christ into their heart and doing so with the upmost of sincerity. Never forget what is written in Philippians 2:10-11(KJV):

> ". . . at the name of Jesus every knee should bow, of things
> in heaven, and things in earth, and things under the earth;
> And every tongue should confess that Jesus Christ is Lord,
> to the glory of God the Father".

By the way, as an afterthought, it should be noted that **prior** to the "Battle of Armageddon" there will be a Third World War where the Bible says more than **two billion** people will be killed. This World War III is brewing as we speak. This war is foretold in Ezekiel 38:1-16. There is too much information within these scriptures to list them here. However, those interested in a detailed breakdown please contact me at the address listed at the end of this book.

In a recent (2015) interview with Mr. James Richards, the CIA's Asymmetric Warfare Advisor, by Money Morning, Mr. Richards is quoted as revealing:

> ". . . that all 16 U.S. Intelligence Agencies have begun to prepare for World War III with Russia and her allies".

The agenda behind World War III is to invade Israel, wipe out the Jewish people, to take a spoil, and to dismantle the U.S.'s "Reserve Currency Status".

According to Bible prophecy this attempt will be squashed by the supernatural intervention of God. Please reference Ezekiel 39:1-4 for details. You can also contact me at the address listed at the back of this book for details.

However, so many will be killed, that this opens the way for Antichrist to come into vogue, and here's the reason why:

Prior to the 1900s, never has there been a war that killed even one million people. However, in World War I, eight million people were annihilated. Then in WW II, fifty-two million were killed. After more than **two billion** are slaughtered as a result of this Third World War, people will say: 'We've had enough! Something must be done to put an end to all this crazy insanity'. And, again, as Paul Henry Spaak declared, ". . . *send us such a man. Be he a god or a devil we will accept him*".

Here comes Antichrist; here comes Antichrist; right down Antichrist lane . . . you get the picture, I'm sure.

This invasion (World War III) is touched upon in the chapter, "The Last World Empire", so I won't detail it here.

Please, let me encourage you to receive Christ Jesus into your heart and do so with real sincerity and not just lip service, because time is running short, and soon these events are going to come to fruition . . . **for all of God's Word comes true.**

There are over 3,000 predictions in the Bible and more than 70% have already been fulfilled in exact detail. Most people are not cognizant that this is so simply because they are indifferent as to what the Scriptures have to share with men. Don't be caught unprepared because, *". . . at a time ye think not, the Son of man cometh"!*

CHAPTER FOUR
VALIDITY OF SCRIPTURE

BEFORE GETTING INTO OUR next chapter the "Last World Empire", we need to address whether or not there is any "validity" to God's Word.

In I Corinthians 2:14 KJV, it states:

> "... the natural man receiveth not the things of the Spirit of God: for they are foolishness unto him: neither can he know them, because they are spiritually discerned".

Therefore, if we are to trust in God's Word, we have to become as "babes", forsaking all our erroneous ideas and notions about the Bible and step forth in faith and simply believe what God says in His Word. Also, in Chapter Eight, "Can We Trust God's Word", I share an article on how our NASA scientists had to trust what the Bible said about a missing day in space in order for the space program to continue. Even still, I realize that many might find it difficult to accept the Scriptures as valid until they have more proof. Just like, Thomas, the apostle, who would not believe that Jesus rose from the dead until he could place his finger into the nail prints in Jesus' hands and insert his hand into Jesus' side where the soldier had thrust a spear, you perhaps require more evidence of the Bible's validity; and that's ok! Hopefully, this chapter will provide what you need in order to do just that.

LOTTERIES

Most people, I'm sure, are familiar with State-run lotteries. In Ohio, for instance, we have a game called the "Super Lotto". The idea is that you must pick six numbers out of a possible 47 numbers to win. On the backside of the "Super Lotto" ticket it states what the chances are of a person winning: in this case it's 10,737,573 to one. That's only one chance in over ten million. With such slim chances of ever winning it makes one wonder why anyone would ever bother playing the lottery in the first place . . . especially when their hard-earned money is at stake.

Now, I personally, have never played a lottery game. I can only imagine what one might feel by taking such chances. The exhilaration of knowing that there might be a chance (even if it is a minute chance) of taking home millions of dollars must be overwhelming for many. For myself, I get an exhilarated feeling knowing that I have a book, the Bible, that contains predictions about life and death and eternity . . . over 3,000 predictions in fact, and whereby over 70% of those predictions have already come to complete fulfillment and in exact detail. To me, anyway, that's a sure thing; undoubtedly, a win-win situation!

For example, during the period from BC 1,000 to BC 500, twenty-five predictions concerning the betrayal, trial, death and burial of Jesus Christ were made by several prophets at different times. All twenty-five of them were literally fulfilled within twenty-four hours by Jesus Christ. Now, I'm no whiz-kid when it comes to math, but I would venture to say that the chances for those prophecies to have been fulfilled has to be in the tens of thousands.

One could possibly say that, if one individual prophet should make several predictions as to some specific event, he could, by collusion with others, bring it to pass. However, when different prophets provide very detailed predictions as to a particular event and they do so over a period of several hundred years, the chance of collusion is not valid. There were over a hundred predictions made concerning Christ that were fulfilled at His first coming over 2,000 years ago. The chance of that happening, as it did, has to be astronomical. Jesus declared in Matthew 5:18 (KJV):

> "For verily I say unto you, till heaven and earth pass, one jot or one tittle shall in no wise pass from the Law [Scriptures], till all be fulfilled". (Brackets mine).

This is an amazing statement and is, itself, prophetic. Although, in truth, we certainly cannot actually prove or disprove the validity of Christ's statement ". . .*until heaven and earth pass*", we can make an honest appraisal of the accuracy of Biblical prophecies by taking several prophetic Scriptures and comparing their accuracy with recorded history.

Breaking down hundreds of fulfilled prophecies would be an endless task. I have, however, picked three outstanding examples in order to establish a precedent for other fulfilled prophecies. I decided on these three for the following reasons:

A.) All three prophecies were predicted by Old Testament prophets, establishing a more than adequate span of time in order to eliminate possible collusion.

B.) All three prophecies predict a great deal of detail which is presented in plain enough English for anyone to interpret. The predictions made by some, like Nostradamus, are vague and strangely worded, but these are not.

C.) All three prophecies have history to back up their fulfillment, and the last prophecy not only has history to back up most of its fulfillment, you and I will undoubtedly witness its final fulfillment in our own time.

Amazed by this? You should be; especially after you read what's coming next!

PREDICTION #1

In Ezekiel 26:3-5, 7, 14, and 16 there's a prophecy concerning the great city of Tyre that was made by Ezekiel back in the year 590 BC. Let's begin now by stating the prophecy:

> "Therefore thus saith the Lord God; behold I am against thee, O Tyrus, and will cause many nations to come up against thee, as the sea causeth his waves to come up. And they shall destroy the walls of Tyrus, and break down her towers: I will also scrape her dust from her, and make her like the top of a rock. It shall be a place for the spreading of nets . . . for thus saith the Lord God; behold, I will bring upon Tyrus Nebuchadnezzar king of Babylon . . . and they shall lay thy stones and thy timber and thy dust in the midst of the water . . . and I will make thee like the top of a rock: thou shall be a place to spread nets upon; thou shalt be built no more: for I the Lord have spoken it, saith the Lord . . . then all the princes of the sea shall come down from their thrones, and lay away their robes, and put off their embroidered garments: they shall clothe themselves with trembling".

First of all, it should be mentioned that Tyrus is the same as the Tyre of today, and this prophecy predicts the destruction of Tyre (Tyrus) and makes the following statements concerning that which would occur:

A.) Nebuchadnezzar, King of Babylon, would overtake the city.
B.) Besides the kingdom of Babylon, other nations would be involved in the destruction.
C.) Tyre would be made flat like a rock.

D.) Fisherman would spread their nets there.

E.) The timber and stones and debris left from the destruction of the city would be laid into the sea.

F.) Because of the fall of Tyre, other cities would become fearful.

G.) The city of Tyre would never be rebuilt nor any other city in its place.

WOW! That's a myriad of details and very unusual detail at that. It will be most interesting to learn more about this prophecy. So let's get to it!

The Phoenicians who inhabited the city of Tyre, located on the coast of Palestine, were a very powerful and greatly feared people. For years King Nebuchadnzzer endeavored to conquer Tyre. It wasn't until 573 BC that he was able to take Tyre. However, everything of value was transported by the Phoenicians to an island some 2,700 feet off the shore of Tyre. The island, itself, was quite impregnable, so although King Nebuchadnezzar did take the city, he gained nothing of real value. As a result, the King withdrew and returned to Babylon. Therefore, item "A" was now fulfilled: for King Nebuchadnezzar did take the city of Tyre. Please be aware that Ezekiel's prophecy was given seventeen years prior to Tyre's destruction.

The Phoenicians never did return to their old city, but remained on the island and built a new city of Tyre. However, because Alexander the Great was concerned about the powerful naval fleet of the Phoenicians, he made other coastal conquests in order to strengthen his own armada. Even with these combined forces he was unsuccessful in conquering Tyre. Finally, he decided to construct a causeway from the mainland to the island in order to make conquest feasible. However, to build this causeway he had to utilize every timber, every brick, every stone and every piece of building material left from the ruin of old Tyre. Even this was insufficient. Therefore, he instructed his men to scrape the ground flat, using the soil down to the bedrock, in an attempt to finish the causeway. Finally, Alexander was victorious and this victory brought items "B", "C" and "E" to fulfillment: "B", other nations would be involved; "C", the city would be made flat like a rock; and "E", its timbers and soil would be laid into the sea.

Neighboring cities were so overwhelmed by the victory that they became very fearful and, without opposition, surrendered. This fulfilled item "F", that other cities would become fearful at the fall of Tyre.

Today, fishermen use the flat rocky ground on which to lay their nets, thus fulfilling item "D", it would become a place for the spreading of nets.

The original city of Tyre has never been rebuilt. This is most surprising for it is a perfect site for a city to be built, and has an exceptional supply of fresh water which is one of the most important requirements for the establishment of a city. Thus far, "G", holds true to the prediction, that Tyre would never be rebuilt.

Please note that although this prediction was made thousands of years in the past, and while it did pertain to those living at the time Daniel predicted it, the prophecy does, indeed, remain true even today.

This is an absolutely astonishing prophecy and I'd be at a loss to determine the chances of it having been fulfilled so accurately. It has to be as great as one of those "Super Lotto" tickets. Just think, if just one prediction in the Bible stands one chance in millions of coming true then, if we were to take all 3,000 predictions and multiply those by a factor of millions-to-one, the probability factor of the Bible being inspired by God is infinitesimal!!! *How can one not believe?* Yet many don't believe because they're unaware of such predictions. And why is that? Simply because people do not care enough to pursue God's Word as so encouraged in II Timothy 2:15 as previously noted.

PREDICTION #2

The second prophecy concerns Palestine and the Jewish people. It consists of two very prophetical statements, both Old Testament prophecies, yet, 904 years apart. I chose these prophecies simply because they eliminate any and all possibility of collusion.

Let's read from Leviticus 26:33-35 (KJV) which was written in 1491 BC and from Ezekiel 36:33-35 (KJV) which was written in 587 BC:

> "And I will make your cities waste, and bring your sanctuaries unto desolation ... And I will scatter you among the heathen, and will draw out a sword after you: and your land shall be desolate, and your cities waste". (Leviticus).

> "Thus saith the Lord God: In the day that I shall have cleansed you from all your iniquities I will also cause you to dwell in the cities, and the wastes shall be built. And the desolate land shall be tilled". (Ezekiel).

The following eight predictions were made:

1.) Palestine's cities would become waste. This, of course, happened in A.D. 70 when the Roman general, Titus, attacked and destroyed Palestine. Thousands of Jews were annihilated.
2.) Sanctuaries would become desolate. This we know occurred because Titus destroyed the Jewish Temple burning it to the ground.

3.) The land would become very desolate. History has shown that because so many Jews were killed and because the Romans had no interest in Palestine at that time, the land became barren and fruitless.

4.) The Jewish population would become scattered. The Romans were relentless. They chased the Jewish people to the four corners of the world. They did not want the Jews to reunite and disrupt the empire ever again.

5.) A sword would go out after the Jews. This refers to persecution, and history verifies that the Jewish people have been, and still are, the most persecuted people on the face of the earth. Even in our civilized societies, anti-Semitism is unbelievable.

6.) The Jews would return to Palestine, rebuild their cities, and once again till their land. We witnessed the fulfillment of this portion of the prophecy in our very own generation. For in1948, with the passing of the Balfour Declaration, the Jews were given back their promised land and they have been building up their cities at an unprecedented rate. Also, they have not only tilled the land, but God has allowed their land to produce abundantly even in dry, arid soil. Their unique irrigation systems and agricultural techniques are truly world renowned.

Never in the past has the land of Israel been so productive as it is today proving that this prophecy is now being fulfilled before our very own eyes.

These two prophecies are quite amazing. It is incomprehensible, to me, that such predictions could be made with such exacting detail unless they were divinely inspired. What is especially interesting is the time span. These prophets had absolutely nothing to gain in their lifetimes by prophesying such things. So what was to be accomplished? God's Will for sure!

God's plan for mankind will encompass several thousand years (implied) and these prophets played only a small part in God bringing everything together. They acted out of "faithful obedience" and "Godly direction". They probably didn't even comprehend their own God-inspired prophecies.

PREDICTION #3

The last prophecy I wish to illustrate is, to me, the most outstanding. History has not only verified the fulfillment of the first nineteen parts of the prophecy, but has also, as of 1981, verified that the foundation has been established for the final fulfillment of the last portion of the prophecy, as you'll soon discover.

This entire prophecy centers around a dream that, King Nebuchadnezzar, the King of Babylon, had been perplexed over. Having called to his aid the magicians, astrologers and sorcerers of his day, to describe and interpret his dream, and all of them having failed to do so, the King then called upon the prophet Daniel. Why Daniel? Daniel was a man of God and highly revered by the people of his time. And, since the King's aides could not interpret his dream (which was punishable by death), he thought that perhaps this man of God could. I'd say that Daniel was placed in a rather precarious position, wouldn't you?

Daniel had great faith that God would not only make known to him the exact dream, but also the interpretation of it, in order that he could meet the King's request. Turning, now, back to the book of Daniel 2:31-45 (KJV), we read:

> "Thou, O king, sawest, and behold a great image, whose brightness was excellent, stood before thee; and the form thereof was terrible.

This image's head was of fine gold, his breast and arms of silver, his belly and thighs of brass, his legs of iron, his feet part iron and part clay.

Thou sawest still that a stone was cut out without hands, which smote the image upon his feet that were made of iron and clay, and brake them into pieces.

Then was the iron, the clay, the brass, the silver, and the gold broken to pieces together, and became like the chaff of the summer threshing floors; and the wind carried them away, that no place was found for them: and the stone that smote the image became a great mountain, and filled the whole earth.

This is the dream; and we will tell the interpretation thereof before the king.

Thou, O king, art a king of kings: for the God of heaven hath given thee a kingdom, power, and strength, and glory.

And wheresoever the children of men dwell, the beasts of the field and the fouls of the heaven hath He given into thine hand, and hath made thee ruler over them all. Thou art this head of gold.

And after thee shall arise another kingdom inferior to thee, and another third kingdom of brass, which shall bear rule over all the earth.

And a fourth kingdom shall be strong as iron: for as much as iron breaketh in pieces and subdueth all things: and as iron that breaketh all these, shall it break in pieces and bruise.

And whereas thou sawesth the feet and toes, part of potter's clay, and part of iron, the kingdom shall be divided; but there shall be in it of the strength of the iron, for as much as thou saweth the iron mixed with miry clay.

And the toes of the feet were part of iron, and part of clay, so the kingdom shall be partly strong, and partly broken.

And whereas thou saweth iron mixed with miry clay, they shall mingle themselves with the seed of men: but they shall not cleave one to another, even as iron is not mixed with clay.

And in the days of these kings shall the God of heaven set up a kingdom, which shall never be destroyed: and the kingdom shall not be left to other people, but it shall break in pieces and consume all these kingdoms, and it shall stand forever.

For as much as thou saweth that the stone was cut out of the mountain without hands, and that it brake in pieces the iron, the brass, the clay, the silver, and the gold; the great God hath made known to the king what shall come to pass hereafter: and the dream is certain and the interpretation thereof sure".

In verse six above, Daniel used the word "we" and one might wonder who "we" represents because only Daniel was speaking. Daniel wanted the king to know that it was God's Spirit speaking through Daniel, to provide the king with the interpretation, and that it was not just Daniel, himself, speaking. This is truly how the Lord works in peoples' lives and how inspiration of the Scriptures comes about.

This type of situation occurred at various times in the Bible. One occasion was when Moses had to stand before the Pharaoh of Egypt and warn him of God's impending plagues. Moses was fearful for he was not a good speaker. God told Moses not to fear because, the Spirit of God, would give Moses the words to speak . . . and He did!

Getting back to Nebuchadnezzar's dream, the illustration below depicts the mighty image the king envisioned. The head was of gold, the breast and arms were of silver, the belly and thighs were of brass, the two legs were of iron, while the feet with the ten toes, were a mixture of iron and clay.

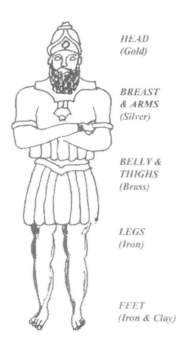

HEAD
(Gold)

BREAST
& ARMS
(Silver)

BELLY &
THIGHS
(Brass)

LEGS
(Iron)

FEET
(Iron & Clay)

This prophecy is broken down into twenty-two predictions. However, we can only consider the first nineteen of them because, as of this time, the twentieth through twenty-second predictions have yet to be fulfilled; but it is possible they soon will be in our generation.

- The probability that Daniel could predict that there would eventually be only four more empires succeeding the Great Babylonian Empire is absolutely astonishing. There could have been a dozen empires; perhaps more. However, the end has not yet come; but we do know that three of the empires have arisen <u>since</u> Nebuchadnezzar's Empire and, exactly as Daniel said they would. These three great empires were: a.) the Medio-Persian Empire; b.) the Grecian Empire; and c.) the Old Roman Empire. The European Empire, (the European Union of today), will be the fourth.

The European Union was made up of ten original nations: Belgium, Holland, and Luxemburg were formed in 1948; then West Germany, France and Italy were admitted in 1957; and finally, in 1973 England, Ireland and Denmark were admitted. In 1981, Greece became the tenth member nation. These formed the base (initial) ten nation/states required in order to set the foundation for Daniel's prophecy of the Last World Empire.

Actually, according to Daniel 7:24 (KJV), there will have to eventually be thirteen member nations. Why? . . .the Scriptures tell us so. After Antichrist takes control of this Last World Empire he will eventually oust three nations bringing the total back down to ten. And, believe it or not, this has already occurred, for Spain was admitted in early 1986 as the eleventh member, Portugal was admitted in the latter part of 1986 as the twelfth member, and Austria was admitted in 1995 . . . thus, your thirteen member nations, of which three will be ousted by the Antichrist. I will expound on this issue of ousting three nations further on in this book.

I must clarify, however, that there is a "fly in the ointment", if you will. Since 1995 there have been some fifteen (15) additional nations admitted into the European Union and this has brought doubts into the minds of many as to the real accuracy of Daniel's prophecy.

Please don't let such deviations sway you from trusting in the validity of God's Word. Here's the story:

Although there are currently a total of twenty-eight member nations in the EU, that will change shortly, and here's why:

The EU is truly in shambles both economically and politically. There is so much confusion going on within the twenty-eight members that major changes are in the making. The leaders of the EU want to merge some member states into single states or nations, similar to what transpired with Greece; for Greece was originally made up of four separate states and this caused many problems. I believe that the current members will be realigned into thirteen nations (probably the original 13), and then, when Antichrist takes control, he will oust three (Denmark, Ireland and Greece . . . I'll explain why these three later), bringing the confederation (EU) back down to ten nations as Daniel predicted. I wouldn't even be surprised if areas like the United Kingdom don't eventually leave on their own and set the stage for other countries in the EU to follow suit. Now let's continue.

- That King Nebuchadnezzar's Empire was the richest empire to ever come into existence has been proven through history. A logical deduction would be that each successive empire would grow in wealth, not decrease in wealth. How could Daniel possibly know this? In any case, when Daniel depicted the head of the image as gold, and that the head represented Nebuchadnezzar's Empire, Daniel was right on the money!

- That a second empire would follow after the Babylonian Empire was not too very difficult to predict. It seems logical.
- That the second empire would be stronger than the first again, is not too difficult to imagine, in that an empire would have to be stronger in order to make conquest.
- That the second empire would not be as rich as the first is considerably less likely. The Medio-Persian Empire was represented by silver in lieu of gold and history clearly tells us that the Medio-Persian Empire was less wealthy than the Babylonian Empire. In order to predict that, Daniel would surely have had to have been divinely inspired.
- That the second empire would be a divided empire is truly an incredible prediction. This was illustrated by the two arms of the image indicating a division in two . . . the Medes and the Persians. It could have been a division of four, as was the case with Greece; or possibly ten, as Daniel predicted for the end-time empire. Also, the Medio-Persian Empire came second in line; why not some undivided empire?
- That the second empire would be larger in land area than the Babylonian Empire is less difficult to predict because the conquering empire would have just gained territory. However, one would think that when gaining territory an increase in wealth would follow. However, this was not the case.
- That a third empire would evolve, is more difficult to predict. Our history books prove that the Grecian Empire came third in line.
- The third empire (the Grecian Empire), represented by the brass in the image, being stronger than the second is a recorded fact. History has shown that Alexander the Great of Greece, had a vast empire and very powerful; it had exceeded any to date.
- That the third empire would not be as rich as preceding empires is certainly more difficult to predict. When one

considers the vastness of Alexander's empire it would seem that he would have had an abundance of wealth, but not so. Sorry, Alexander!

- That the third empire, the Grecian Empire, would be vastly larger than its predecessors is logical to me. However, having said that, while Daniel is predicting larger empires as time goes on, he's also predicting empires less wealthy, and that is seemingly out of character in the equation. Yet, that's what good old Daniel did, and he was correct (or should I say, the Lord?).

- That a fourth empire would come into existence is increasingly more difficult to predict. How far in advance could one conceivably see concerning the birth of empires? Yet, Daniel proved himself once again.

- That the fourth empire, the Roman Empire, would be stronger than the third, as iron is stronger than brass, is quite interesting because during Daniel's day the Babylonian Empire was considered to be the ultimate in strength and wealth, and how much stronger could an empire get. Good for you Daniel.

- That the Roman Empire would not be as rich as Alexander's empire would be very, very difficult to predict so far in advance. Nonetheless, God inspired Daniel and Daniel followed through.

- That the Roman Empire would be a divided empire is unbelievable. And, that the division would be in two is even more outstanding. Why not a division in four, or six, or ten? History shows that at the end of the Roman Empire's rule it was divided into the Eastern and Western divisions. Gosh, Daniel, you're batting 100%!

- This prediction indicates that a fifth empire will arise. <u>We are now living at the time of this fifth empire.</u> It is represented by the feet with the ten toes which scholars believe represents the European Union; and I concur wholeheartedly. The feet and toes are made up of a combination of iron and clay, for these nations have the iron of despotism and the clay of Democracy.

- That the end-time empire would consist of a final ten nations combined into a single working unit is intoxicating to say the least. With the creation of the EU this appears to be very possible. Only time will tell the whole story.

- That the end-time empire would not be as wealthy as the Roman Empire, the Grecian Empire, the Medio-Persian or the Babylonian Empire doesn't even register to my way of thinking. This last world empire covers an area that represents most of Europe, and that is huge, and there should be a great deal of wealth involved here; but, apparently, this isn't going to be so.

- Lastly, that the end-time empire would be partly strong and partly weak, as the iron and clay mixture illustrates, is truly amazing. The EU does, indeed, exhibit a partially strong, partially weak character. The EU is torn between its democracy and its struggle for unification.

Please note as well, that at the end of Daniel's prophecy it says:

> "For as much as thou saweth that the stone was cut out of the mountain without hands, and that it brake in pieces the iron, the brass, the clay, the silver, and the gold; the great God hath made known to the king what shall come to pass hereafter: and the dream is certain and the interpretation thereof sure".

The stone mentioned above is Jesus Christ; for Jesus Christ is referred to as the cornerstone in Scripture, and He will come back with the Saints at the "Battle of Armageddon" to finish breaking into pieces all the kingdoms of mankind before setting up His own kingdom during His Millennial Reign.

The probability that all nineteen predictions out of twenty-two would be fulfilled just as stated is so astronomical, it boggles the imagination.

The European Union had to evolve sooner or later because of Europe's economic decay. Mr. Winston Churchill, following World War II, warned that the future salvation of Europe depended on political union, for I quote:

> "Our main theme of salvation should be the Grand Alliance
> of the European powers".

Jean Monnet, who is referred to as, the "Father of Europe", had the same dream; and it was he who helped create the European Union; although it was called the Common Market in days past. The idea was to establish a united free Europe without national boundaries which would bring about a gigantic empire larger than the United States of America or Russia.

Considering this concept of a united Europe, one cannot help but wonder about Daniel's prophecy of an end-time empire consisting of ten nations united into a single Confederacy.

It's also interesting to note what was predicted in Daniel 2:44 (KJV):

> "In the last days of these kings shall the God of heaven set
> up a kingdom which shall never be destroyed".

Did you catch it? Daniel said that in the Last Days of these ten kings, (the ten kings who will rule over the ten nations/states), God will set up His Kingdom!

Another reason to consider that this European Union will consummate all world governments and bring about Christ's Kingdom here on earth can be comprehended by using God's "Mathematics in Scripture" (reference chapter six with the same name). As you'll learn, the number ten, according to God's "Mathematics in Scripture", represents worldly completion. That is something one should definitely give thought to.

As I mentioned earlier on, there are over 3,000 prophecies in the Bible and more than 70% have already been fulfilled in every detail and with unequivocal accuracy. Without exception, history can verify their fulfillment. The idea is this: If the Bible can make so many accurate predictions with the probability of their having been fulfilled so astronomical, that it staggers the imagination, should we not all begin giving God's Word some earnest consideration and attention? If one can take a chance on a "Super Lotto" ticket, why not take a chance on the Bible? You're sure to win if you do.

CHAPTER FIVE
THE LAST WORLD EMPIRE

It's time now to discuss an extremely important situation which, as of this writing, is currently developing in Europe. As we begin, please keep in mind, that when I say, "The Last World Empire", I mean the last world empire that mankind will establish here on earth; for God will set up His own kingdom (empire) during His Millennial Reign (which is a period of 1,000 years that will <u>begin</u> after the Battle of Armageddon; and a time where Christ Jesus rules the world under a dynamic Theocratic form of government).

If you remember when I discussed, the "Validity of Scripture", that mention was made of Daniel's prophecy of the "seventy weeks", and that the seventieth week commences the "Tribulation". It will initiate Antichrist's coming into vogue where he takes complete control of the ten-nation Confederacy which will encompass most of the territory of the Old Roman Empire.

I don't mean to be overly redundant; however, as you might also recall, King Nebuchadnezzar had a very perplexing dream and he had called upon Daniel to interpret it for him. Daniel did so and he explained to the king that after his kingdom (which was represented by the head of gold on the image of the warrior), that a second empire, the Medio-Persian Empire, would come into existence; then followed by the Grecian Empire; followed yet again by the Roman Empire; which, ultimately, was the strongest that ever existed. Then Daniel told the king that a "Last World Empire" would evolve, consisting of ten nations united into one. These ten base nations are:

A.) Belgium

B.) Holland

C.) Luxemburg

D.) West Germany

E.) France

F.) Italy

G.) England

H.) Ireland

I.) Denmark

J.) Greece

I had also mentioned how, in actuality, there would have to be a minimum of thirteen member nations in this Confederacy because, according to Daniel 7:24, this end-time ruler, Antichrist, will eventually subdue (or uproot, oust) three of the member nations because they're "troublesome", and they will resist the agendas of the Antichrist. Three additional nations were admitted into the Confederacy prior to 1995. They were:

K.) Spain

L.) Portugal and,

M.) Austria

Fast forward to 2016 and what do we have in place? First of all, there are currently twenty-eight member nations, not thirteen, in the EU; so what gives? As noted in the chapter on, "Validity of Scripture", it was stated:

> "The European Union is truly in shambles both economically and politically. There is so much confusion going on within the twenty-eight current members that major changes are in the making. The leaders of the EU want to merge some of the members into single states or nations (similar to what transpired in Greece in the past, for Greece was divided

into four separate states after Alexander's death and this caused many problems politically and economically). I believe that current members will be realigned into thirteen nations, and then, when Antichrist takes control, he will oust (subdue, uproot) three of the members who resist this new formation".

All any of us need do is watch today's news: CBS News, Fox News, World News, etc., to realize that the EU is in dire turmoil and there are talks in session, even now as I'm writing this book, that a major **"restructuring effort"** of current member nations is being considered in order to establish a much sought after economic and political stability.

What all the leaders of the European Union are planning is anyone's guess, but I can assure you that this Confederacy will, eventually, become a thirteen nation Confederacy, and will remain so until Antichrist makes his debut. Keep in mind that it will be Antichrist, himself, who will subdue three of the nations, for we read in Daniel 7:24 (KJV):

> *"And the ten horns out of this kingdom are ten kings that shall arise: and another shall rise after them; and he shall be diverse from the first [first ten kings and the nations under their control], and he shall subdue three kings".* (Brackets mine).

The ten horns which Daniel speaks about in the above verse are the same as the ten toes on the image of the warrior in King Nebuchadnezzar's dream. In the above verse where it says, *". . . and another shall rise after them; . . .",* this "another", is none other than the Antichrist.

Antichrist will not come forth from the base ten nations in the original prophecy, but rather, he'll come forth from a nation outside of the original ten, for when Daniel talks about, *". . . and he shall be diverse from the first [first ten kings] . . .",* that means he'll come forth from a nation other than the original ten. It's very possible that Antichrist could come from either: Spain, Portugal, Austria or, perhaps, even Syria, (just a hunch on my part, however). So keep your eyes and ears open.

You just might be asking, "Why are the ten last world nations being represented by both the ten toes of King Nebuchadnezzar's dream as well as ten horns on the beast in another of Daniel's prophecies? Hey, guys, it's just the way God does things. Let's just say that it adds intrigue to the mixture. Heck, why not? If movie producers can do such things, God certainly can? I just thought that I'd add that tidbit to satisfy your curiosity.

Today we are living at a time when knowledge is increasing exponentially and we can comprehend things today that Daniel, and his peers, could never grasp. That's why the Lord told Daniel:

> *". . . shut up the words, and seal the book, even to the time of the end: many shall run to and fro, and knowledge shall be increased".*

We have greater knowledge today of the universe, for example, than the prophets of by-gone days could ever have dreamed possible (although I do believe that there is sound Scriptural evidence that a pre-Adamite civilization existed . . . people who lived on earth prior to Adam's and Eve's time . . . who had even greater knowledge than we have in many areas which I address in the chapters under "Great Mysteries"). With today's technology we can envision possibilities unfolding which would have been most difficult for the prophets of the Old Testament to comprehend.

Another prophecy of Daniel's (that didn't concern King Nebuchadnezzar), which is instrumental in predicting and end-time, ten-nation empire, can be found in Daniel 8:8-9, 21-23. I will not confuse you by stating those verses, for they are difficult to understand. But let me just say this:

Daniel predicted that the Grecian Empire would be divided into four parts (Daniel 8:8). This was fulfilled after the death of Alexander the Great when four of his generals decided to seize Alexander's empire and divide it as follows:

A.) General Cassander took all of Greece and Macedon.
B.) General Lysimachus took Asia Minor, or present day Turkey and Thrace.
C.) General Seleucus took all the eastern parts including the states of Syria, Iraq, and Iran (modern day nations).
D.) General Ptolemy took the kingdom of Egypt. Palestine became a buffer state between Syria and Egypt who waged war with one other for some 150 years ending in 165 BC. Antiochus Epiphanes, king of Syria, reigned at that time.

All of these divisions except for the eastern part of the kingdom of Seleucus, were conquered by the Romans and they became part of the Old Roman Empire. These four separate divisions of Greece were: Turkey, Syria, Greece and Egypt. I cannot see, however, that Turkey, Syria and Egypt will be a part of the revised Old Roman Empire of the last days. I feel, however, that perhaps Antichrist could possibly come forth from Syria (but that is another book for another time).

Why am I proposing that the ten-nation, end-time Empire will come forth from the area of the Old Roman Empire? The reasoning is that in King Nebuchadnezzar's dream of the warrior image, he envisioned the two legs of iron blending into the feet with ten toes made up of iron and clay and it is interesting to note that all, except one, The Old Roman Empire were destroyed by invading armies. The Old Roman Empire was never really defeated militarily; it perished from deep within; leaving open the possibility that it could one day become revised (and that's what Daniel is predicting with the interpretation of the King's dream).

I've led you to believe that this European Union will be the Last World Empire that men will ever govern . . . well, this isn't quite true. The truth of the matter is, there will ultimately be a sixth empire; and this sixth empire will be a "Revised European Union"; still comprising the ten nations, but which Antichrist will take final control of and claim for himself. It will last for only three and one half years (the second half of the Tribulation). Please note that this "sixth" empire established by Antichrist is also represented by the number of "man" (which is six . . . "6"). This confirms that this empire will be the last empire that mankind will ever establish, because the seventh empire is established by Christ Jesus and seven in Bible language is the number of perfection (refer to Chapter Six, Mathematics in Scripture).

Before Antichrist can accomplish this he must, however, subdue the three troublesome nations previously mentioned which are Denmark, Ireland and Greece, for in Daniel 7:25 (KJV), we read:

> "And he [Antichrist] shall speak great words against the most High, and shall wear out the saints of the most High [they are those individuals who will be saved during the Tribulation, **not** those who have already been raptured], and think to change times and laws: and they [three nations] shall be given into his hand until a time and times and a dividing of time". (Brackets and bold lettering mine).

It will take Antichrist and his forces three and one half years to defeat these three opposing nations in order to establish this final sixth kingdom; at which point, Antichrist, will celebrate his victory by entering into the newly built Jewish Temple (the Jewish Temple will be rebuilt during the first 3-1/2 years of the Tribulation period) and will defile the Jewish Temple by proclaiming to be a god and eliminating all Jewish sacrifices and oblations.

How do we know that this conquest of the three nations will entail 3-1/2 years? In the above verse of Scripture it says: ". . . *and they shall be given into his hands until a time and times and a dividing of time*". A time, in Scripture, represents one year; and times is equal to two years; and a dividing of time equals one half year: Totally, that equates to 3-1/2 years.

Also, how do we know that the "They" in the above Scripture means the three troublesome nations? When the expression "given into" is used it means to surrender. The only ones who surrender to Antichrist after 3-1/2 years are the three nations in question.

A similar expression is utilized in Revelation 17:12-13, but in a different context. In this verse, those who are doing the "giving" are the ten nations; however, that verse also states that "These have one mind, and shall **give** their power and strength unto the beast": they do so freely because they are of one mind. The three nations in question, however, "give into" (surrender) to Antichrist; but do so against their will.

Once the Antichrist defeats these three nations he will have created his own "European Union Empire", just as Daniel predicted. This time, there will be only the one king ruling over this revised European Union Empire . . . Antichrist! How can one know this? In Revelation 17:12-13 (KJV), it is spelled out quite clearly:

"And the ten horns which thou sawest are ten kings, which have received no kingdom as yet; but receive power as kings one hour with the beast [Antichrist].

These have one mind, and shall give their power and strength unto the beast [the Antichrist]". (Brackets mine).

The subduing of these three nations is verified in Daniel 7:18 where it states:

". . . he shall uproot three nations (kings)".

What's truly amazing is that three of the original ten nations in the EU have caused trouble almost from the very beginning. These three nations are: Ireland, Denmark and Greece. As proof that these three nations have been "troublesome", I would like to share with you these following articles:

April 1, 1985, Arab News: "Ireland, the only member state outside NATO, rejects possible cooperation in defense and security within the community, as do Denmark and Greece".

September 7, 1985, The Economist: "A new Dutch text attempts to straddle remaining differences with an ingenious let-out clause on security issues that could satisfy neutral Ireland, legalistic Denmark and halfhearted Greece".

January 3, 1987, The Economist: ". . . Last-minute hitches in Ireland and Greece delayed ratification of the reform of the Rome Treaty".

July 9, 1988, Jerusalem Post: "The intifada is responsible for some diplomatic setbacks. It was either the direct cause, contributory factor or the convenient excuse for the following:

"The failure of Greece to keep its promise to raise diplomatic relations with Israel to embassy level . . .

Ireland's continuing refusal to accept Israeli ambassador in Dublin.

. . .When President Dhaim Herzog visited Denmark last November, pro-Israeli feelings in that traditionally sympathic country were at an all-time high. Now they are at an all-time low, with . . . anti-Israeli demonstrations and wall graffiti becoming an almost daily feature in Copenhagen street life . . ."

We see that these three nations are contrary to NATO and to any defense and security measures by the European Union: most importantly, they are also contrary to Israel.

This is powerful. When Antichrist comes on the scene, one of the first things on his agenda is to confirm Israel's seven-year treaty. With Ireland, Denmark and Greece being opposed to all of the above mentioned, as well as, being contrary to Israel's support, it is a certainty that Antichrist will no doubt have to subdue (oust, uproot) these three nations.

Hey folks, it's right around the corner. Since the posting of these articles things among Ireland, Denmark and Greece have certainly escalated. And, although these articles were posted some twenty-five years ago, in the scheme of things, that represents very little time.

The Bible says: To God, a thousand years is as a day, and a day, as a thousand years. Bible Prophecies are being fulfilled, and they are being fulfilled quickly!

So then, how are things lining up? First of all, we have the original ten nations/states inside the EU: Belgium, Holland, Luxemburg, West Germany, France, Italy, England, Ireland, Denmark and Greece. Then Spain, Portugal and Austria joined the EU prior to 1995. These thirteen base nations fulfill Daniel's prophecy up through 1995. Since then some fifteen other nations joined, making the current number of nations in the EU twenty-eight; however, and as previously explained, these fifteen will most likely get absorbed into the original thirteen (or other nations will leave). Once this "absorption" process takes place, the EU will be a more stable union with thirteen nations. It's interesting to note that the number thirteen is a demonic number. Just a thought to pass on to you.

When Antichrist finally makes his debut, he will go to war with Ireland, Denmark and Greece in an attempt to oust (subdue, uproot) them from the Confederacy. It will take Antichrist three and one half years to accomplish. At that point there will be left ten nations headed by ten kings just as Daniel prophesied. Then, and in celebration of his victory, he decides to enter into the new Jewish Temple proclaiming himself to be a god; stated as the "abomination of desolation" in Scripture; and he will, at that time, break his peace treaty with Israel and endeavor to annihilate the Jewish race. Antichrist's effort will be unsuccessful due to the supernatural intervention of Almighty God. This will anger the Antichrist to such a degree (because he knows his time is going to be short-lived), that he lets loose his wrath upon all of mankind. He will do so for 3-1/2 years. Then God will defeat Antichrist and put an end to all things at the "Battle of Armageddon"; the last and final battle in which mankind will ever engage.

It's all forming just as the Holy Scriptures have foretold. It's happening now as I write this book, and all anyone needs to do is to compare today's news headlines with what I've presented, and the light of truth will shine bright!

Keep your eyes looking upward, for as Matthew 24:44 so aptly puts it:

> "Therefore, be ye also ready; for in such an hour as ye think
> not the Son of Man [Jesus Christ] cometh". (Brackets mine).

Don't be fooled, in Matthew 16:3 (KJV), Christ rebuked all the Sadducees and Pharisees (Jewish teachers) of His day saying:

> "O ye hypocrites, ye can discern the face of the sky; but can
> ye not discern the signs of the times?".

What were these "signs of the times" that Jesus Christ spoke about? Simply that Christ Jesus, their Messiah, the Son of God, was now among them bringing salvation and truth to all men. Today, Jesus Christ is saying to all of us:

> "O ye hypocrites, ye can discern the face of the sky; but can
> ye not discern the signs of the times?".

The signs of the times are staring us in the face. Can we not see them for what they are? We can if we see with our eyes, and hear with our ears, and feel with our hearts what the Lord God is showing us and telling us!

Let me digress from our discussion on the Last World Empire just for a moment and delve into why mankind can't seem to get things right.

People are strange. Quite often it appears as though anything people find hard to believe or comprehend, they either reject it as being possible or, if they feel it is possible, but just not clear to their understanding, they simply set it aside and refuse to even think about it. People have many preconceived ideas and notions and anything that confronts those ideas and notions is classified as a "No-no!", and is scoffed at. God's Holy Word is a good example of what I'm saying. Many claim to know something about Scripture, but they really don't. People will simply wander around aimlessly not knowing what to believe or think because such matters as "religion", so they say, should be kept private (which is a fallacy according to the Bible), and God's Word gets pushed into the back of a closet to collect dust and no one has to be any the wiser.

The Bible is one of the most misunderstood books simply because it has to be studied and not just read. It truly amazes me how often I see a Bible in someone's home and when I ask them about it, they have little to say. To many, it's only a status prop.

Many will spend a great deal of time studying those things that will satisfy their bodies, and little, if any time, studying those things which can satisfy their spirits. This is stated in II Corinthians 2:14 (KJV), which says:

> "But the natural man receiveth not the things of the spirit of God: for they are foolishness unto him: Neither can he know them, because they are spiritually discerned".

Anything of value must be earned. To be able to understand Scripture takes much study and the working of God's Holy Spirit within the individual. Finis Jennings Dake, in his book entitled, "God's Plan for Man", expressed this sentiment quite well, for we read:

"Jesus constantly invited and provoked study of the Scriptures, and even rebuked men for their lack of knowledge of revealed truth. He attributed all error to a lack of knowledge of the Bible. He answered His critics by saying 'Ye do error, not knowing the Scriptures, nor the power of God' [Matthew 22:29 KJV]. He commanded men to, "Search the Scriptures, for in them ye think ye have eternal life, and they are they which testify of me' [John 5:39 KJV].

. . ."Peter speaks of the 'unlearned and unstable, twisting the Scriptures to their own destruction' [II Peter 3:16-18 KJV]. However, no person belongs to this class if he will make up his mind to believe and obey what is written, instead of rebelling against it".

God's Word is for every individual. It's for anyone who will renew his mind, open up his heart and surrender his will to God. When this is done, God will enlighten that person with more truth than he has ever known before! Those that claim that they cannot understand the Scriptures are those who do not want to take the time to understand. They only want to understand those things that interest them and, for so many, their spiritual lives have little interest to them. Spiritually, they're dead!

The Scriptures tells us of such people. They are the "so-called" wise and prudent personages with, possibly, a great deal of book knowledge, and perhaps practical experience to go along with their book knowledge, but their minds and their hearts are closed: They look to themselves and man for answers, and certainly not God. Aside from God's self-imposed limits when dealing with men, God is unlimited in every respect. Man is a very limited creature; therefore, his knowledge and experience are limited. There is no limit to God's knowledge, so why do men depend largely upon themselves rather than God? The answer, Pride!

I've been subjected to persons who claim that they have been all through the "religion bit" and say you can't believe half of what you hear. In a way, I can sympathize with these individuals, for I've been in their shoes myself. Having said that, however, I can also tell you that there is an innate quality in each and every one of us, letting us know there truly is a God of love, who enables us to understand His truth. Proverbs 2:1-6 (KJV) says:

> "…if thou will receive my words, and hide my commandments with thee; So that thou incline thine ear unto wisdom, and apply thine heart to understanding; Yea, if thou criest after knowledge, and liftest up thy voice for understanding; if thou seekest her as silver, and searchest for her as hid treasures;Then shalt thou understand the fear of the Lord, and find the knowledge of God. For the Lord giveth wisdom: out of His mouth cometh knowledge & understanding".

Please don't fall into the following trap:

> "This people's heart is waxed gross, and their ears are dull of hearing, and their eyes they have closed; lest at any time they should see with their eyes and hear with their ears, and should be converted, and 1 should heal them". (Matthew 13:10-17 KJV).

Every person needs to know what God is warning mankind as it relates to these last days. We need to trust in His Word so that we can all prepare our hearts for the soon return of His Son. God forbid that we do not!

My hope is that, after you have considered what is being presented in this book, you will understand the implications, and that you would, at the very least, give Jesus Christ a chance in your life.

Getting back now to our discussion of this Last World Empire, it is imperative that we look into what Christians and Bible scholars accept as the most important sign indicating the soon return of Jesus Christ.

Let's start by quoting a Scripture from the book of Matthew 24:32-34 (KJV), and then follow through with Ezekiel's prophecy as found in Ezekiel 37:1-12 (KJV):

> "Now learn the parable of the fig tree; when his branch is yet tender, and putteth forth leaves, ye know that summer is nigh:
>
> So likewise ye, when ye shall see these things, know that it [the end] is near, even at the doors . . .".
>
> Verily I say unto you, this generation shall not pass, till all these things be fulfilled." (underscore mine).

What generation was Jesus referring to and, what are those things that will transpire during that generation?

The generation that Jesus was referring to, is that generation beginning as of 1948, when the Jews took that initial step to re-establish themselves once again as a nation. I previously discussed that this reestablishment of the Jewish Nation was made possible when Great Britain passed the Balfour Declaration, giving Palestine back to the Jews. **This is the most notable sign of the nearness of Christ's return!**

In the book of Ezekiel 37:1-12 (KJV), we find that God instructed Ezekiel to prophecy about this re-gathering of the Jewish people:

> "The hand of the Lord was upon me, and carried me out in the spirit of the Lord, and set me down in the midst of the valley which was full of bones, and caused me to pass by them round about: and behold, there were very many in the open valley; and lo, they were very dry, And He said unto me, son of man, can these bones live? And I answered, O Lord God, thou knowest.
>
> Again He said unto me, Prophesy upon these bones, and say unto them, O ye dry bones, hear the word of the Lord. Thus saith the Lord God unto thee bones; Behold I will cause breath to enter into you, and ye shall live: And I will lay sinews upon you, and will bring flesh upon you, and cover you with skin, and put breath in you, and ye shall live; and ye shall know that I am the Lord.
>
> So I prophesied as I was commanded: and as I prophesied, there was a noise, and behold a shaking, and the bones came together, bone to his bone. And when I had beheld, lo, the sinews and the flesh came up upon them, and the skin covered them above: but there was no breath in them.
>
> Then said He unto me, Prophesy unto the wind, Prophesy, son of man, and say to the wind, Thus saith the Lord God; Come from the four winds, O Breath, and breathe upon these slain, that they may live.

> So I prophesied as He commanded me, and the breath came
> in unto them, and they lived, and stood up upon their feet,
> an exceeding great army.

> Then He said unto me, son of man, these bones are the
> whole house of Israel: behold, they say our bones are dried,
> and our hope is lost: we are cut off for our parts. Therefore,
> prophesy and say unto them, Thus saith the Lord God;
> Behold, O my people, I will open your graves, and bring you
> into the land of Israel".

This is a powerful prophecy. Some of you might be thinking that
this prophecy is too in-depth for anyone to determine if it means
what I claim it means. Please do not be disturbed by this; for unless
one devotes the time and effort to study, it would be very difficult to
understand its meaning. However, this is why I'm writing this book:
". . . ye shall know the truth, and the truth shall set you free".

What can be really helpful in understanding such Scriptures are the
background materials on the history of the Jewish people.

For instance: To know that the nation of Israel was conquered and
the people dispersed twice in past history; once by the Babylonians
in 586 BC, and then again by the Romans in 70 AD; and then to
relate Ezekiel's prophecy to a time after the Jews were dispersed by
the Romans (or for the second time); and then to know from history
that Israel never did come back together again as a Jewish nation
until the 1948, really says something.

The second to last verse brings together what is being prophesied,
for God said to Ezekiel:

> ". . . these bones are the whole house of Israel".

Now we can relate to that which the figurative language is referring (the whole house of Israel). Then it says of the Jews:

"... Our bones are dried, our hope is lost: we are cut off for our parts".

This was an expression of the Jews towards God, after their second dispersion, when the Romans had scattered all the Jewish people throughout the world, and how His people cried unto Him because of their dire situation. This prophecy was not only given for the benefit of mankind today as a guide to the last days, but to reassure the Jews that not all is lost, and that one day they would surely be brought back to their promised land.

The more background material one has, the more history one studies, and the more one gets use to the flow of Scripture, the easier it is to follow what is being expressed. However, the most effective measure for determining whether or not certain prophecies have been properly interpreted is to verify the accuracy of their fulfillment, and this we did in earlier chapters.

This re-gathering of the Jewish people back to their homeland, which was firmly established over 68 years ago, is most significant in the fulfillment of prophecies yet to be fulfilled in our generation. We now have the expanded knowledge; sufficient enough to understand that God's Prophetic Word always comes true; all we need do is believe.

It is very important to bring into focus different Scriptures as they relate to certain thoughts, ideas and predictions. For example: How do we know that this re-gathering of the Jewish people to their homeland means the end is near? Can't this be a prediction that one day the Jews would inhabit their land again, but not necessarily in the last days? The answer is an emphatic, NO! We must search the

Bible for other Scriptures as they pertain to this event of the Jews coming together again and see how they all stack up.

An example of what I'm sharing is found in Ezekiel 38. Ezekiel is talking about how God told him to prophesy concerning an invasion of Israel. This particular invasion could not occur until the Jews returned back to their homeland (after the second dispersion by the Romans); and, until 1948 the Jews have been a scattered people. Therefore, students of the Bible know that this invasion could not happen until the Jews were safely back in their promised land, and this is what the Antichrist will accomplish when he confirms the seven year covenant with Israel. Now, we must ask ourselves, "Are there any Scriptures which would indicate when this invasion would take place?" We find the answer in Ezekiel 38:8, and 11-12 (KJV) which states:

> "After many days thou shalt be visited: in the latter years thou shalt come into the land that is brought back from the sword, and is gathered out of many people, against the mountains of Israel, which have been always waste: but it is brought forth out of the nations, and they shall dwell safely all of them".
>
> And thou shalt say, I will go up to the land of unwalled villages; I will go to them that are at rest, that dwell safely, all of them dwelling without walls, and having neither bars nor gates,
>
> To take a spoil, and to take a prey . . .".

These Scriptures explain that this invasion will be during the "latter days" (which, in the Bible, is synonymous with the "last days", "end times", etc.). These verses also verify that it is only the Jews being addressed because of, references made to: ". . . and brought back from the sword", which is only related to the Jews and Israel; ". . . and is gathered out of many people . . .", which is indicative only of the Jewish race; ". . . against the mountains of Israel . . .", which is quite clear as to where, etc. All such verses begin to stack up and clarify what is being said.

And, again, don't forget Matthew 24:32-34 which relates the parable of the fig tree as noted below:

> "Now learn the parable of the fig tree; When its branch is yet tender, and putteth forth leaves, ye know that summer is nigh;
>
> So likewise, when ye shall see all these things, know that it is near, even at the doors.
>
> Verily I say unto you, This generation shall not pass, till all these things be fulfilled.
>
> Heaven and earth will pass away, but my words shall not pass away." (Brackets mine).

The parable of the fig tree is symbolic of the Jews "budding" once again in their homeland and illustrating that when all the things which were brought to light in Matthew 24 occur (which is known as the "Olivet Discourse"), then would we know that the end is very near.

And what were the things that Matthew stated would occur in the latter of days? It states in Matthew 24:4-14:

> "Take heed that no man deceive you.

THE LAST WORLD EMPIRE

For many shall come in my name, saying, I am Christ: and shall deceive many.

And ye shall hear of wars and rumors of wars: see that ye be not troubled: for all these things must come to pass, but the end is not yet.

For nation shall rise against nation, and kingdom against kingdom: and there shall be famines, and pestilences, and earthquakes, in divers places.

All these are the beginnings of sorrow.

Then shall they deliver you up to be afflicted, and shall kill you: and ye shall be hated of all nations for my name's sake.

Then shall many be offended, and shall betray one another, and shall hate one another.

And many false prophets shall rise, and shall deceive many.

And because iniquity shall abound, the love of many shall wax cold.

But he that shall endure unto the end, the same shall be saved.

And this gospel of the kingdom shall be preached in all the world for a witness unto all nations; and then shall the end come".

And, yes, we have experienced many wars, pestilences, famines, earthquakes, etc., and all throughout history. What is really being expressed here, however, is that when all such things as these occur with greater intensity, more often, and all at one time . . . then will the end come!

And, what generation exactly will it be that will experience all these things and usher in the last days? You guessed it; our very own generation; since we are witnesses to this re-gathering of the Jews to their national homeland.

While we're talking about the Jews re-gathering to their homeland, consider this: The rate of return is absolutely phenomenal. Since 1900 there were only 50,000 Jews living in Palestine. By the mid-twenties there were 84,000. By the thirties there were 175,000. However, ever since the passing of the Balfour Declaration in 1948, the influx of Jews escalated some 400% that very first year and by more than 800% by the year 1952. Today, there are some 4,000,000 Jews living in Palestine. And, as the Bible states: 'when the fullness of times comes about, all hell will break loose . . . literally!'

The next chapter, "Mathematics in Scripture", will provide some background on how God works. Hopefully, it will enable you to better understand upcoming chapters.

CHAPTER SIX
MATHEMATICS IN SCRIPTURE

THE LORD HAS A plan for everything. Everything God does, He does by number, by weight, and by measure.

There is a "Time System" revealed in the Bible which Bible scholars have called the "Weeks of Scripture". There are seven such weeks:

1.) Week of days
2.) Week of weeks
3.) Week of months
4.) Week of Years
5.) Week of Weeks of Years
6.) Week of Millenniums
7.) Week of Ages

As author of the Scriptures and Creator of the world, God had to make certain that His Word harmonized with all His Works and, indeed, they do. For example, the seven "Weeks of Scripture" noted above are common in nature:

> "The hen sits three weeks, the pigeon two, after having laid eggs for two weeks. The ova of salmon are hatched in 20 weeks. Of 129 species of Mammalia, the majority have a period from conception to birth of an exact number of weeks. The same is true of the human race. Fevers and intermittent attacks of gout, ague and similar complaints have a "Septiform Periodicity", and the Seventh, Fourteenth

and Twenty-First days in certain diseases are known as "critical days". Then there are seven notes in the musical scale, seven colors in the rainbow, seven rays in prismatic light, and the leaves of plants are largely governed in their form by the same law of sevens".

This harmony of Nature with Scripture is not a mere coincidence either and verifies that both were Divinely conceived.

This same harmony is also revealed by various numbers throughout Scripture as well, and is symbolized as follows:

- One . . . number of "Unity"
- Two . . . number of "Union"
- Three . . . number of "Divinity"
- Four . . . number of the "World"
- Five . . . number of "Division"
- Six . . . number of "man"
- Seven . . . number of "Perfection"
- Eight . . . number of "The New Order of Things"
- Ten . . . number of "Worldly Completion"
- Twelve . . . number of "God's Eternal Perfection"
- Forty . . . number of "Probation"

Please take special note of the number SIX, for it is the number of man. It is my belief that the idea behind the "666" being the Antichrist's number, is that man (represented by "6"), is made up of body (6), soul (6), and spirit (6) . . . in other words, the total aspect of man; and man is endeavoring to deify himself . . . and Antichrist . . . who represents the ultimate abomination of man, will never reach "seven", or perfection. The saving blood of Christ Jesus is the only thing that makes men righteous in God the Father's eyes.

Item 4, "Weeks of Years", are the weeks given in Daniel's prophetic vision of the "Seventy Weeks", (reference back to the chapter titled, Tribulation & Armageddon). With a week representing seven years in his prophecy, then the 70 weeks would actually constitute 490 years totally. The first 69 weeks would figure out to 483 actual years; with one week left, of seven years, yet to be fulfilled. This last seven year period will be the time span for the Tribulation.

For those of you who feel that Jesus Christ is not coming back, consider this: God truly does work speedily, for time does not exist for Him. The Bible says in II Peter 3:8 (KJV):

> "But, beloved, be not ignorant of this one thing, that one day is with the Lord as a thousand years, and a thousand years as one day".

Yes, God is longsuffering toward us, but He will not be mocked. In Galatians 6:7 (KJV), it states:

> "Be not deceived; God is not mocked: For whatsoever a man soweth, that shall he reap. For he that soweth to the flesh shall of the flesh reap corruption; but he that soweth to the Spirit shall of the Spirit reap life everlasting".

It is my personal belief that there is adequate evidence in the Scriptures indicating that God has a plan for mankind that will last for seven thousand years (God's number for perfection). We are rapidly approaching the end of the first six thousand years, and the last one thousand years will involve the "Millennial Reign of Christ Jesus". So please, be on guard, because the Tribulation, the Battle of Armageddon and the return of Christ, where He actually places His foot upon earth once again, (like He did back over 2,000 years ago), will all transpire prior to Jesus Christ's "Millennial Reign" (or the seventh thousandth year).

I cannot say this enough: Please ask Jesus Christ into your heart before it's too late. The truth is there . . . receive it!

Remember that the Bible states:

"Today is the day of salvation"
Don't wait!

CHAPTER SEVEN
THE RAPTURE

AT THIS POINT, I need to explain about an event referred to as the "Rapture". This is an event spoken about in the Scriptures which deals with all the "Believing Christians" being removed from the planet prior to the last seven years on earth, known as the Tribulation period.

<u>This event is probably the most encouraging and hopeful promise given Believers by God in the Bible.</u> Having said this, however, it does need to be clarified to avoid confusion.

There is some debate as to the exact timing of the Rapture. The majority of Christians believe in a "Pre-Tribulation" rapture event. There are some who believe in a "Mid-Tribulation" rapture; and then, there are a very select few who believe in a "Post-Tribulation" rapture. And, still again, there is a minority who believe that the rapture occurs at one's appointed time of death. So what's the story here?

I won't get into the reasoning of those who believe that the rapture will occur "Post-Trib" or at the actual time of death. I'll let them defend their own thinking on the matter. I will, however, like to present why I tend to believe in a "Pre-Trib" rapture and explain why I find it difficult to support a "Mid-Trib" rapture.

Let's start by looking into what the Bible has to say concerning this great event. Before doing so, I must state that the word "Rapture" is not found in the Bible. It only describes an event noted in the Scriptures. I Thessalonians 4:13-18 (KJV) states:

> "But I would not have you to be ignorant, brethren, concerning them which are asleep [dead], that ye sorrow not, even as others have no hope. For if we believe that Jesus died and rose again, even so them also which sleep [have died] in Jesus will God bring with Him. For this we say unto you by the Word of the Lord, that we which are alive and remain unto the coming of the Lord shall not prevent them which are asleep [dead]. For the Lord Himself shall descend from heaven with a shout, with the voice of the archangel and with the trump of God: and the dead in Christ shall rise first: Then we which are alive and remain shall be caught up together with them **in the clouds, to meet the Lord in the air:** and so shall we ever be with the Lord. Wherefore, comfort one another with these words". (Emphasis and brackets mine).

Some have asked me why do the dead in Christ rise first? Well, I'm not God, therefore, I do not have any real answer to that question. I will say this, however: Perhaps it's because the dead have six feet farther to travel when we're all taken up into the clouds. Just kidding!

At this juncture I need to clarify something which has been greatly misunderstood. Most individuals are familiar with the expression: "The Second Coming of Jesus Christ". However, there are three actual "comings" of Jesus Christ mentioned in the Bible. Christ's first coming was in the flesh . . . over two thousand years ago. Then there is a "Second" coming of Christ, referred to as the "Rapture". Most Christians believe this event will precede the Tribulation Period. The third "coming" of Jesus Christ is where the confusion reigns. The most commonly referred to "Second Coming" occurs at the end of the Tribulation period where Christ literally comes back to planet earth and places His feet upon the ground. With this particular "coming", Jesus Christ, and the raptured Saints, come back to earth to destroy Antichrist and his armies at the final battle of "Armageddon"; and immediately Christ sets up His Millennial Reign (a period of 1,000 years designed to test the faithfulness of those who come through the Tribulation alive).

The "Second Coming" of Christ, which most Christians refer to as the "Rapture", is found in I Thessalonians 4:13-18 (KJV), as noted above; but is also mentioned in I Corinthians 15:51-54 below, for I quote:

> "Behold, I show you a mystery: We shall not all sleep [die], but we shall all be changed, in a moment, in the twinkling of an eye, at the last trump: for the trumpet shall sound, and the dead shall be raised incorruptible, and we shall be changed. For this corruptible must put on incorruption, and this mortal must put on immortality. So then when this corruptible shall put on incorruption, and this mortal shall put on immortality, then shall be brought to pass the saying that is written, death is swallowed up in victory". (Brackets mine).

These Scriptures (I Thess. 4:13-18 and I Corth. 15:51-54) depict an event, the "Rapture", in which Christ does come, but He doesn't place His feet to the ground. Christ will come only in the clouds (I Thessalonians 4:17) where all believers will be meeting with Him. It is my position (as it is with most Christians) that this "Rapture" will occur prior to Christ's last coming back to earth at the "Battle of Armageddon"; and sometime prior to the Tribulation period.

Please be aware of the fact that the differences in viewpoints concerning the exact timing of this event is not due to contradictory Scriptures or because scholars cannot seem to interpret them properly. It is simply because there are really no Scriptures which indicate the exact year and time in which this event will occur. All we can do is "guesstimate", if you will, by bringing all pertinent Scriptures together and try and make sound sense of them. The "Rapture" is a certainty; however, the exact timing is open for debate as to it being a Pre-Trib., Mid-Trib., or a Post Trib. event.

Let me briefly explain why some believe in a Mid-Tribulation rapture so that when I provide you support for a Pre-Tribulation rapture you might better appreciate where I'm coming from.

The Bible mentions a select group of individuals who will act as witnesses for Christ during the first half of the tribulation and this group is known as the "Manchild". Since the "Manchild" is a group of Jewish believers; and since the Bible states that they get "raptured" during the middle of the tribulation; the Mid-Trib. theorists claim that that signifies a mid-trib. event which includes all believers, not just the "Manchild" group.

The problem I see with this theory is that the "Rapture" is actually an event designed for the "Church of Believers", not the "Manchild". The "Manchild" consists of 144,000 witnesses, made up of 12,000 Jewish believers from each of the twelve tribes of Israel; and, because they are witnesses for Jesus Christ they are actually believers. However, they are a "select" group of believers, and not part of the actual "Church of Believers", as such. Think of it this way: The Jews were God's "<u>Chosen</u> People" back since the beginning of mankind. Also, anyone who accepts Jesus Christ as their Lord and Savior, is <u>chosen</u> by God for salvation. What you have here are two separate groups of "chosen" people. Both groups are "chosen", as it were, yet, they are different; and will be dealt with differently.

The "Manchild" should be considered separately from the "Church of Believers". This is why the "Manchild" group is raptured separately, and during the middle of the Tribulation; whereas the "Church of Believers" is delegated to be raptured prior to the Tribulation period. The "Manchild's" purpose is to act as witnesses for Christ; whereas the actual purpose of the "Church of Believers" is to experience the promise of God that He would: "keep Believers from the trials to come", as shown in Revelation 3:10 (KJV) below:

> "Because thou hast kept the word of my patience, I also will **keep thee from** the hour of temptation, which shall come upon all the world, to try them that dwell upon the earth". (Bold emphasis mine).

The "hour of temptation" mentioned above is the actual Tribulation period.

The "Church of Believers" will have done their part during God's "dispensational period of grace" by accepting Jesus Christ as their Lord and Savior. Now it's God's further plan and purpose for the "Manchild" to preach the gospel of Jesus Christ to all the non-believers that are left behind. God's "chosen people", the Jews, failed to do this in the past, and they still do continue to rebel. This will definitely change, however, by God's decree!

In Daniel's prophecy of the Seventy Weeks, only the Jewish nation and Israel are being dealt with. This prophecy, although it is pertinent to all Christians because it does determine the nearness of Christ's return, it certainly does not concern any of the "Gentile Christians"; only the Jews. As a result, the "Manchild's removal from the earth during the middle of the Tribulation should be looked upon as a separate happening from the removal of the Gentile/Jewish Christians, (the "Church of Believers), prior to the Tribulation.

God's "Chosen People" (Jews), and God's "Church of Believers", are two separate and distinct groups and God will deal with each group accordingly. Since most of the Jews did not receive Jesus Christ as their true Messiah, God then turned to the Gentiles with His offer of salvation. The Gentiles received Christ with open arms and, thus, became the "Church of Believers", as well as all those Jews who also believed in Christ for salvation. The "Church of Believers", also referred to as the, "Church of Christ", will also become the, "Bride of Christ". . . because of their belief. All saints, of all ages, will become a part of the "Bride of Christ". In addition, all Tribulation martyrs will become a part of the "Bride of Christ" (Revelation 7:1-17; 14:1-5; 15:2-4, and 20:4-6). According to Hebrews 11:8-16 (KJV), the Old Testament saints will also be a part of the "Bride of Christ"; and according to Hebrews 13:14 (KJV), the present day saints will be a part of the "Bride of Christ". In short, every company of redeemed (saved) people will become, and are, the "Bride of Christ".

As mentioned earlier, there will actually be three raptures (removal of believers). The first rapture will consist of all believers (both living and dead) from the time of Adam and Eve to the end of the Church Age, (which ends immediately and prior to Antichrist coming on the scene). This is called the "Rapture" that we are mostly concerned with and is one of the major events bringing hope to the Christians today. There will also be the "rapture" of the "Manchild" in the middle of the Tribulation. And lastly, there will also be the "Rapture" of any Tribulation Martyrs just prior to Christ's final return to earth at the end of the Great Tribulation period. So please keep this thought in mind as we continue.

First, I would like to give you II Thessalonians 3:3 (KJV), which states:

> *"But the Lord is faithful, who shall stablish [establish] you,*
> *and keep you from evil". (Brackets mine).*

This verse follows Paul's discussion of the end times. It was meant that Believers during the last days should have this wonderful hope; not only for themselves, but also, that Believers might be a testimony to non-believers . . . and that hope is: God will keep Believers <u>from the trials</u> to come during the Tribulation.

Even Jesus indicated that true Believers would escape the terrible things that would transpire during the Tribulation, because in Luke 21:34-36 (KJV), we read:

> *"Pray that ye may be accounted worthy to escape all these*
> *things that shall come to pass, and to stand before the Son*
> *of Man [Jesus Christ]". (Brackets mine).*

To what things was Jesus referring? Namely, the things outlined in Matthew chapters 24 and 25; Luke 21:1-19; and all of Revelation chapters 6-18. I won't list those verses here for lack of space, but you might wish to refer to them. Some of things listed in these chapters are: wars, rumors of war, famines, pestilences, diseases, both natural and supernatural disasters, the mark of Antichrist, religious persecution, economic collapse, and the dictatorial leadership by the most demonic of men . . . Antichrist!

Revelation 3:10 (KJV), also declares:

> *"Because thou hast kept the word of my patience, I also will*
> ***keep thee from*** *the hour of temptation, which shall come*
> *upon all the world, to try them that dwell upon the earth".*
> *(Bold emphasis mine).*

The "hour of temptation" spoken of here is the Tribulation. Please note that this verse clearly states that: "*. . . I will keep thee <u>from the hour</u> of temptation . . .*"*!* That precise form of expressing something is most interesting, for what it's actually implying is that: I, the Lord your God will not bring you through the trials, but rather, I will **keep you from** the trials to come. That's a very huge difference, my friends, and certainly, most encouraging!

I believe that the following Scripture verse spells out quite clearly that "true Believers" will be removed from planet Earth just prior to the Tribulation. II Thessalonians 2:6-8 states:

> *"And now ye know what withholdeth that he [the Man of Sin – Antichrist] might be revealed in his time. For the mystery of iniquity doth already work: only he who now letteth will let, until he [the Spirit of God working through the Believers] be taken out of the way. And then shall the wicked [Satan working through the Antichrist] be revealed, whom the Lord shall consume with the spirit of his mouth, and shall destroy with the brightness of His coming . . ."* (Brackets mine).

I can appreciate that these verses can be a bit disconcerting for many without some explanation as to what's being said. Therefore, I will endeavor to do so as gracefully as I possibly can.

"And now ye know what withholdeth . . ." is the **"key"** to this verse. The Spirit of the Lord, working through the true Believers, is what is doing the withholding. That which is being withheld is the revelation of the "Wicked One" . . . or, Antichrist. The Spirit of God working through the Believers is keeping Satan from being exposed, and also, from fulfilling himself through Antichrist. Once the true Believers have been removed, mainly evil-minded people and non-believers will remain. When this happens, Antichrist will find humanity,

"easy pickings", if you will, since all resistance, at least for the most part, will be eliminated. Most of the non-believers who will be left behind will not necessarily be evil-minded, but more simply, non-believers: people who held to the attitude of, who cares! It is for this particular group that the Tribulation will have its most rewarding effect. Those who refuse to accept Jesus Christ prior to the Tribulation, while there is still time, will most likely come to the realization that they have made a very BIG mistake by not accepting Jesus Christ into their lives. Once they do see the truth (and the error of their ways) they will most assuredly seek Christ out. Chances are it will cost many of them their lives (since they will have refused the Antichrist), but they will gladly do so, now that they have seen the true light. The Lord will provide these new believers with all the strength and courage necessary to do what needs to be done; even to the giving up of their lives.

There is still another reason to believe in a Pre-Tribulation Rapture: There is simply no reason for Believers to experience the trials to come. Right now mankind is living in a period which is referred to as "Grace". During this period of grace, God is giving mankind time to repent and come back to Him and receive His Son, Christ Jesus, as their Lord and Savior. Anyone who does receive Christ into their lives, will not only benefit by being granted eternal life, but will be "kept from" the trials to come. There is no need for a Believer to suffer the tribulation to come because the main purpose for the Tribulation is to inspire people to repent. If one already believes, then he doesn't have anything for which to repent because Jesus died for man's sins. We just have to believe that.

Some might say that Believers in past history suffered many trials and even death for their beliefs, so why should Believers living today be exempt from persecution?

That was so because God's plan for mankind still had a long way to go before its fulfillment. Now things are quite different. There is little left to be fulfilled under God's timetable. He is going to cut off His providential hand of grace upon mankind and let Satan have his way. God has provided ample warning for us in order to get our lives in order. Take heed, while there is still time left.

God does not need true Believers to be around to act as witnesses to non-believers who enter into the Tribulation. The Lord will have sealed the 144,000 Jews to act as witnesses, for in the book of Revelation 7:4 (KJV), we read:

> "And I [John] heard the number of them which were sealed: and there were sealed an hundred and forty and four thousand of all the tribes of Israel".

The reason that 144,000 Jews will be sealed is so Satan (working through Antichrist) cannot have them martyred.

In addition, in Revelation 11:3, John writes about the two witnesses of God who will testify in the streets of Jerusalem for three and one half years and these two witnesses will not be sealed, and will, after three and one half years, be martyred. For it states:

> "And I [God] will give power unto my two witnesses, and they shall prophesy a thousand two hundred and threescore days, clothed in sackcloth". (Brackets mine).

These two witnesses will be given supernatural power in order to cause things to happen that are so astonishing that many unbelieving Jews and Gentiles will finally turn to Christ. The two witnesses will prophesy for 1,260 days, or for the first half of the seven year Tribulation. At this point, Antichrist will have them martyred and will leave their dead bodies in the streets of Jerusalem for three full days. However, after the three days have passed, God will resurrect them (as He did Jesus), and receive them into heaven. This act, too, will bring many to Christ.

Who are these two witnesses you might ask? No one is actually certain as to exactly who they might be, but we do believe that Enoch, an Old Testament prophet, will be one. There is some debate about the second witness. Some say Elijah the prophet; others say Moses. I am of the belief that the two witnesses will be Enoch and Elijah. I say this because neither of these prophets ever experienced physical death; they were "translated" directly into heaven. The Bible says:

> "It is appointed unto men once to die, and then the judgment".

Since Enoch and Elijah never suffered physical death, then it makes sense that when they come back to act as witnesses, they need to die in order to fulfill Scripture, and God always fulfills His Word!

Moses' death is, however, in question. After he led his people into the promised land, God did not allow him to follow the people. Moses was told to remain behind, and there are no records as to how he died or if, like Enoch and Elijah, was possibly translated directly to heaven.

Those that tend to believe that Moses will be the second witness, do so because both Enoch and Moses were seen at Jesus Christ's transfiguration (the event where Christ ascended into heaven). Whichever is the case, there will definitely be two witnesses, preaching in Jerusalem, during the Tribulation; proclaiming that Jesus Christ is the longed for Messiah.

Supporters of the Mid-Tribulation theory say that one needs to refer to Matthew 24:40-41, where it talks about how one out of every two people will be taken away in the middle of the Tribulation, for we read:

> "Then shall two be in the field; the one shall be taken, and the other left. Two women shall be grinding at the mill; the one shall be taken, and the other left".

Mid-Tribulation theorists use this scripture in support of their position. Personally, I can't see that as applying, for the following reason.

To say that two will be in the field, and one taken, and the other left; and two shall be grinding at the mill, and one taken, and the other left; implies that half (or 50%) will be raptured. How can this possibly be since only 2% to 3% of the world's population even believes in Christ Jesus as their Lord and Savior. Matthew 22:14 notes: *"For many are called, but few are chosen"*. Fifty percent of even those left behind during the Tribulation are not what I would call a few.

I tend to believe that this verse simply means that half the population of the world will be destroyed as a result of earthquakes, famines, pestilences, wars, natural disasters and strange supernatural type events.

Consider the following: It has been estimated that by 2017 (or there about) there will be seven billion people on earth. In Revelation 9:18 it states that one third, or approximately 2.3 billion people, will be killed, for we read:

> "By these three was the third part of men killed, by fire, and by smoke, and by brimstone . . ."

Sounds pretty much like a nuclear holocaust to me! Continuing onward, we find that if 2.3 billion people are killed, that would leave 4.7 billion people. However, we also find that in Revelation 6:8 (KJV), it says:

> "And I looked, and behold a pale horse: and his name that sat on him was death, and hell followed him. And power was given unto them over a fourth part of the earth, to kill with sword, and with hunger, and with the beasts of the field".

A fourth part of the remaining 4.7 billion is 1.18 billion people. If you have seven billion people on earth by 2017 and, if per chance, the Tribulation began around that time, and if 2.3 billion die as a result of Revelation 9:18, and 1.18 billion die as a result of Revelation 6:8, what does that represent . . . approximately 49.6%? How close can one get to 50% when dealing with such large numbers? It seems awesome to me!

Please know I'm not trying to purport that the Tribulation is going to begin in the next year or two. Personally, I do believe there are too many additional prophecies that need to be fulfilled first before this time period can begin. However, having said that, I sincerely believe that we are very, very close.

Even high ranking officials in our government Intelligence Agencies are apparently preparing for a possible Third World War. In an article from Money Morning Reports, dated April 8, 2015, it states the following:

> " . . . Should the rise of conflicts across the Middle East and Ukraine serve as a warning that something much more dangerous is approaching?

> . . . *According to Jim Richards, the CIA's Asymmetric Warfare Advisor, the answer is yes.*
>
> *In a startling interview he reveals that all 16 U.S. Intelligence Agencies have begun to prepare for World War III.*
>
> *Making matters worse, his colleagues believe it could begin within 6 months".*

What more can be said? And yes, folks, there will definitely be a WW III, for the Bible indicates such: and according to Scripture it will be headed up by Russia along with her allies. I can't go into detail about what the Bible says concerning this Third World War, for that would take a book of its own. I will say this, however; I strongly believe that this WW III will result in the 2.3 billion individuals who are to be killed, according to Revelation 9:18, and that this war will most likely be fought just prior to the Tribulation. NOTE: This WW III will not be the "Battle of Armageddon". Armageddon will be its own war and the final war on earth. Also, I personally disagree with Mr. Richard's colleagues that this war might start within six months. Why? There are other prophetical Scriptures that must be fulfilled before this war. These additional prophecies can come about very quickly. Therefore, one should not dismiss that thought.

Getting back to my efforts supporting a Pre-Tribulation Rapture, let me share this: If we know from what John says in the book of Revelation that the Antichrist appears at the start of the Tribulation, and if, as Paul states, the wicked one (Antichrist) cannot appear until the "Church of Believers" is removed from the face of the earth; then we can also know, with a fair amount of accuracy, that the Rapture will occur prior to the Tribulation. This fact alone should be incentive enough for people to turn to Jesus Christ now!

If we were to follow my line of thinking, it would agree with the Scripture that says: *"But of that day and hour knoweth no man, no, not the angels of heaven, but my Father only"*. Why? With my way of thinking the Rapture could occur at any time between now and when Antichrist hits the news; leaving the time element left wide open. However, if one were to believe as do the Mid-Trib. theorists, one could know 3-1/2 years prior to the Rapture occurring, by virtue of the fact that, if the Rapture occurs in the middle of the seven years, then all one would have to do is count forward 3-1/2 years starting from when the Antichrist's appearance is made known.

I would also wish for you to consider Revelation chapter 4:1 (KJV). This is very important because starting in chapter four, John, is taken up in the spirit into heaven and shown what would come to pass during the Tribulation:

> "...Come up hither, and I will shew [show] thee things which must be hereafter"...(Brackets mine).

What things were they that Jesus was going to show to John? In the book of Revelation, chapters 6-18 it describes all the many terrible things which would befall mankind, and some of these things I've already brought to light earlier. Now, what's extremely important to notice when reading these verses is the fact that not once is the "Church of Christ" (the Believers) even mentioned. Why? The way I see it, the Believers have already been raptured into heaven prior to these events occurring.

I realize that some readers may say, "Look, Paul made these predictions back in the first century A.D. and the event still has not happened". Who's kidding who?

Please understand that God's plan for mankind encompasses several thousand years, and at the time Paul spoke these things, more than half of God's plan had already taken place. Christians in those days were well aware of the fact that much more Scripture was required to be fulfilled before Jesus could return. And remember what II Peter 3:8 (KJV), proclaimed:

> "But, beloved, be not ignorant of this one thing, that one day with the Lord is as a thousand years, and a thousand years as one day".

The early Christians back in John's day knew that the Lord existed in a "timeless" state and that their purpose was to be prepared, with joy in their hearts; for Christ's return was certain, but not necessarily imminent in their life time.

CHAPTER EIGHT
CAN WE TRUST GOD'S WORD?

THINK FOR A MOMENT and ask yourself, "Where did life begin?" There are only two answers to this question:

A.) Man's theories, or
B.) God's Word

If you decided on man's theories, "Big Bang" or otherwise, you still don't get an answer. If it's the "Big Bang", we need to ask, what initiated the "Big Bang" in the first place? Or, if you go with the concept of extraterrestrials experimenting with life on planet earth, then you need to ask, "Where did the extraterrestrials come from?

Forty-five years ago I had made the decision to honestly confront this issue face-to-face and the choice between placing my trust completely in mankind, or God, had to be determined. There was no middle ground . . . it was either man or God!

I had, up to that point, established my life on what man had to offer with little emphasis on spiritual things. This, however, did not sit well with me; for my inner being was crying out for greater truth, understanding and peace. I felt that I had to either disprove the existence of God and the validity of His Word, or be bound to both, totally and completely. If I could prove that man created such a being as a crutch for his own inadequacies, it would free me to set a course for my life based on what mankind had to offer. By the same token, if I could prove that God does exist and that the Bible is truly God's inspired Word, then I would direct my life accordingly.

When you're a teenager, brought up in a fairly well-to-do family, with many great aspirations of becoming someone important, and with your whole life ahead of you: with love, sex, money and status awaiting the taking; thus, providing the impetus needed for achieving great things, God is the last thing on your mind . . . at least I would have thought that to be true . . . but I was wrong!

What I have come to understand and believe is that God truly does exist and that the Bible is, without question, the inspired Word of God.

This understanding did not come easily due to my pride; nonetheless, I was determined to find the truth. As a result, I began studying the Scriptures with an honest and open heart. One of the first Scriptures that impressed itself heavily upon my heart was in I Corinthians 2:14 (KJV), which says:

> "But the natural man receiveth not the things of the Spirit of
> God: for they are foolishness unto him: neither can he know
> them, because they are spiritually discerned".

Please, funnel in on, **"spiritually discerned"**, for that was the key enabling me to understand God's truth. The physical man will try to resist spiritual truth because spiritual things seem quite foreign to him. That's where the Lord's promises come into focus: Enabling one to understand spiritual matters. However, we do need to "renew our minds and open our hearts", asking God to reveal Himself to us.

This whole concept became clearer after I read Matthew 11:25 (KJV):

> "I thank thee, O Father, Lord of heaven and earth, because Thou hast hid these things [truths] from the wise and prudent, and hast revealed them unto babes . . ." (Brackets mine).

At the very moment I had asked the Lord to loosen the shackles binding me from understanding His revealed truth, so that I could believe, my study became fruitful. As a result, what I have come to understand and believe has completely changed my life, and it will change yours; if you so desire.

And, yes, as a Christian I still do experience trials which confront me day by day. In fact, I have greater trials because now the forces of darkness press against me trying to destroy my faith. Trials do have their advantage, however, for they do build character and strengthen the inner man.

Knowing now my purpose in this life, and those things awaiting me in the next life, I can forge ahead, regardless of the difficulties, knowing with much confidence that which Paul stated in II Corinthians 4:16-18, is true:

> ". . . though the outward man perish, yet the inward man is renewed day by day. For our light affliction, which is but for a moment, worketh for us a far more exceeding and eternal weight of glory; While we look not at the things which are seen, but at the things which are not seen: for the things which are seen are temporal; but the things which are not seen are eternal".

There is always sound foundation to all truth and understanding. If we endeavor to accept these foundations, everything else will unfold before our very eyes. Matthew 6:33 (KJV), does clarify this point:

> "But seek ye first the kingdom of God and His righteousness,
> and all these things [truth, wisdom, understanding, peace,
> prosperity, etc.] will be added unto you. (Brackets mine).

The foundation then, to discovering truth, is to honestly and earnestly seek God with an open mind and heart. Let the Lord strip away the "natural man" and allow His Spirit to work in union with your spirit. Jeremiah 29:13 (KJV), states:

> "And ye shall seek Me, and find Me, when ye shall search for
> Me with all your heart".

And Matthew 6:21 (KJV), backs up Jeremiah's words with:

> "For where your treasure is, there will your heart be also".

You cannot honestly and earnestly seek God if your heart is full of ungodly things . . . and that is a truth you can take to the bank!

We need to know if God's Word's is trustworthy. Well, one way is to do what is described above. However, I realize that for some this is not enough reassurance. Therefore, I would like to share a following true account, as it was told by a Mr. Harold Hill, the President of the Curtis Engine Company, in Baltimore, Maryland, and consultant in the space program:

> "I think one of the most interesting things that God has for
> us today happened to our astronauts and space scientists
> at Greenbelt, Maryland. They were checking the position of
> the sun, moon and planets out in space, where they would
> be 100 years and 1,000 years from now. We have to know
> this so we don't send a satellite up, and in terms of the life

of the satellite and where it will be, so that the whole thing will not bog down.

They ran the computer measurement back and forth over the centuries and it came to a halt. The computer stopped and picked up a red signal, which meant that there was something wrong either with the information fed into it or with the results as compared to the standards. They called in the service department to check it out and they said, 'It's perfect'. The IBM head of operations said, 'What's wrong?' 'Well, we have found there is a day missing in space in elapsed time.' They scratched their heads. There was no answer.

One religious fellow on the team said, 'You know, one time in Sunday School they talked about the sun standing still'. They didn't believe him, but they didn't have any other answer so they said, 'Show us'.

So he got out his Bible and went back to the book of Joshua where they found a pretty ridiculous statement for anybody who has common sense. 'Fear them not, I have delivered them into thy hands; there shall not a man of them stand before thee'. Joshua was concerned and if darkness fell, they [Joshua's enemies] would overpower him.

So Joshua asked the Lord to make the sun stand still [as proof of God's Word]! That's right! The sun stood still and the moon stayed . . . and hasted not to go down about a whole day.

The space men said, 'There is the missing day!' Well, they checked the computers going back into the time it was written and found that it was close, but not close enough! The elapsed time that was missing back in Joshua's day was 23 hours and 20 minutes . . . not a whole day. They read the Bible and there it said, 'about a day'.

These little words in the Bible are important. But still they are in trouble because if you cannot account for 40 minutes you will be in trouble 1,000 years from now. Forty minutes had to be found because it can be multiplied many times over in orbit.

Well, this religious fellow also remembered somewhere in the Bible where it said that the sun went backwards. The space men told him he was out of his mind. But they got out the book and read these words in II Kings, Chapter 20: Hezekiah on his death bed was visited by the prophet Isaiah who told him he was not going to die. Hezekiah did not believe him and asked for a sign as proof. Isaiah said, 'Do you want the sun to go ahead ten degrees?' Hezekiah said, 'It's nothing for the sun to go ahead ten degrees, but let the shadow return backwards ten degrees'. Isaiah spoke to the Lord and the Lord brought the shadow ten degrees backward'. (II Kings 20:10-15 KJV).

Ten degrees is exactly 40 minutes! Twenty-three hours and twenty minutes in Joshua, plus 40 minutes in II Kings make the missing 24 hours the space travelers had to log in the log book as the missing day in the universe'.

Don't you think that if it was good enough for our scientists to log into their computers that it's good enough for us to at least give God's Word a try? Perhaps, if two supposedly ridiculous and mythical statements found in the Bible were true and accurate, others might be also? Think about that carefully.

To avoid confusion, I would like to set things straight concerning the Bible being the inspired Word of God. If people only had understanding of what inspiration truly means, they would be much more relaxed in dealing with the Bible. But for some reason many people do not comprehend what inspiration by God is really all about. As a result, they do let minor discrepancies affect their believing God's Word.

Inspiration, as I've come to understand it, does not mean that in each and every instance God dictated every word the way He wanted them to be written (although in many cases He did). All inspiration means is that God revealed His Word to men, allowing men to express it in their own creative ways, while at the same time, making certain His Word was kept within the boundaries of truth.

Perhaps there are a few instances wherein a translator might have mistranslated a word or two, or perhaps there are a few instances where the facts don't seem to always coincide; but, nonetheless, the truth is there. For example:

Let's say that you and I saw a car swerve out of control and hit a pole. And, assume that we are called upon to report what we saw. You state that a yellow Chevy went out of control and hit a pole. I indicate that a gold Camero lost control and hit a pole. The basic truth here is that a car lost control and crashed into a pole. In both reports the truth can be determined. The immaterial facts of "yellow" versus "gold", and "Chevy" versus a "Camero", have little bearing on the real truth. Besides, "yellow" to some, can mean "gold" to others; and the car in question is both a "Chevy" and a "Camero". Thus, any of the discrepancies and contradictions which one might think are relevant in debating the validity of the Bible, are of such a nature that they do not interfere with the foundational truths which God wanted men to understand. This, combined with the fact that some people simply do not want to believe what is written, does tend to make understanding God's Word difficult.

Please understand also, that the first available English translation of the Bible was the 1611 King James Version. Back then there were not as many English words to describe an idea, a thought, or a concept. One English word, for example, might have multiple meanings and only the context in which the word is used can determine its actual meaning; we will touch on this issue further in the chapters covering "Great Mysteries". If one does not consider all texts depicting a thought, that thought could be interpreted differently by different people.

This is why study of the Scriptures is vitally important. That's why the Lord tells Believers to "search" for His truth earnestly. If one is not interested in truth, then forget it, and suffer the consequences. However, if you are someone who desires truth, then search for it diligently!

Because the Holy Bible bases its authenticity and authority on prophecy, it is very special when comparing it to all other sacred books. No other sacred book contains predictions as to the future . . . only the Bible. If other sacred books employed the use of prophecy, their non-fulfillment would have surely discredited their writings. Fulfilled prophecy is the strongest evidence for inspiration and authenticity than anything else. This is why you will never find another sacred book that employs prophecy.

One can't play guessing games where prophecy is concerned: Prophecy is actually history written beforehand, and to guess future history, and be correct, would be lethal for anyone . . . but not so for God.

One-third of the Scriptures are prophetic in nature. More than half of all the Old Testament prophecies and practically all the New Testament prophecies certainly concern events yet future.

Some individuals might point out that others, such as Nostradamus, for example, have made dozens of predictions which seem to have been fairly accurate and have put their predictions in written form as well. So how can I say that the Bible is the only book to do so?

First of all, I stated that the Bible is the only sacred book to do so. Nostradamus and others did not write sacred books. Then there is the problem that many of the predictions of these physics have never come true and some have left people with the sense that they might have touched on reality, but most of the predictions these physics make, however, cannot really be proven and are so vague that people tend to read into them what they want to read into them. The Bible truly does have history to back up every prophecy, ever made, by any prophet.

Satan is the greatest of all deceivers. According to the Bible, he even deceives God's very own elect. Nostradamus and others, I believe, have been used by Satan . . . probably without their even knowing it. If these physics had their visions from God, then all their predictions would be 100% accurate . . . and, they are not! Neither would their predictions be so vague, as most are.

Satan will do all that he can to dispel the validity of God's Word in order to discourage mankind from trusting in Him. Satan deceived Adam and Eve and he is still deceiving people today. Adam and

Eve were surely no dummies, according to the Bible, but highly intelligent. So, be on guard; if Satan could have deceived them, how about you.

Well, can we trust God's Word? God says that He holds His Word above Himself, and that's good enough for me.

CHAPTER NINE

WHY FAITH?

Jesus states the following concerning the day and hour of His return:

> "But of that day and hour knoweth no man, not the angels of heaven, but my Father only."

Why didn't God the Father make known to men the day and the hour of Jesus Christ's return? The Scriptures tell us in Ephesians 2:8-9 (KJV), that:

> "For by grace we are **saved through faith**, and that not of ourselves: it is a gift of God: not of works, lest any man should boast". (Bold emphasis mine).

If, therefore, we are saved through faith, then how could we have faith if something that was made known to us before time; and, then, how could we ever be saved? Hebrews 11:1 (KJV), says:

> "For faith is the substance of things hoped for, the evidence of things not seen".

According to this verse, faith is the "substance of things hoped for"; in other words, faith is the essence of hope. Without hope, we are lost! God is letting us know that He is our hope. He is the "evidence of things not seen". We must endeavor to trust in the Lord totally and completely with everything (no matter how difficult it is). Proverbs 3:5-6 (KJV) states:

> "Trust in the Lord with all thine heart: and lean not unto your own understanding. In all ways acknowledge him, and he shall direct thy paths".

Personally, I have found this to be one of the most difficult lessons of my life. But I can tell you this: after more than 50 years of learning, I've become victorious!

What enabled me to appreciate God was what I learned from Romans 1:19-20 (KJV):

> ". . . that which may be known of God is manifest in them [men]; for God hath showed it unto them [men]".

> For the invisible things of him [God] from the creation of the world are clearly seen, being understood by the things that are made, even his eternal power and Godhead; so that they are without excuse". (Brackets mine).

How beautiful are these verses. What these verses are saying is that we can know God because He has manifested Himself to each of us (in part, like in the "Introduction" about 'laminins'). How? By all the things which the Lord has made, which are expressions of who He is, and that the invisible things are also clearly seen through that which the Lord has created; even to the extent that there is no excuse for our not seeing them. All one has to do is open his eyes, study the things God has made, and simply believe in the wonder of it all.

Remember, the Bible says that, *"we are saved through faith"*; faith in what? Faith in Christ Jesus. The Bible also says, *"Faith without works is dead"* (James 2:20 KJV). So how does one put his faith in Jesus

Christ to work? The same way you would put the faith you have for anything to work . . . by expressing it openly, honestly, and from the heart. Simply step out and do it.

Have you ever been fearful of doing something and because of that fear you held back. As a result of refraining from stepping out in faith, you never truly came to know the positive outcome there might have been. Many people live their entire lives in such fear. As Mr. Winston Churchill once said: "The only thing to fear, is fear itself". Faith, however, overcomes fear. Step out in faith by accepting Jesus Christ as your Savior. Let your faith be released in order that you should develop a personal relationship with Christ and experience His peace that, *"passeth all understanding"*.

Faith is extremely important to God. In fact, the Bible says, without faith, we cannot please Him; for in Hebrews 11:6 (KJV), it states:

> "But without faith it is **impossible** to please Him [God]: for he that cometh to God must believe that he is, and that he is a rewarder of them that diligently seek him". (Emphasis and brackets mine).

God has fantastic rewards for those who put their trust in Him. The Lord desires to bless His Saints with wondrous things; most of which are beyond our comprehension.

It is your heart and will that God wants. If you can give Him your heart and will, while being confronted by the perplexities of life here on earth, certainly you will give your heart and will to Him when He finally removes all pain and suffering, and tears and sorrows, in the next life. He will replace all the pain and suffering with nothing but unbelievable peace, and joy, and untold blessings.

By believing in Jesus Christ, you are trusting in what He has promised you in His Word; and remember, God holds His Word above Himself: so He can and will fulfill that Word.

You might be thinking, "Faith is all good and fine, but how does one get this kind of faith?" Glad you asked; for in the next chapter, "How to know God", we will explain just how one does that.

CHAPTER TEN

HOW TO KNOW GOD

Most people, at one time or another, will look up into the night skies and wonder about creation, the universe, and life; and where they fit into the scheme of things. When I look up to the heavens I recall Paul's words in Romans 1:19-20 (KJV):

> "Because that which may be known of God is manifest in them [men]; for God hath showed it unto them [men]. For the invisible things of Him [God] from the creation of the world are clearly seen, being understood by the things that are made, even His eternal power and Godhead; so that they are without excuse . . ." (Brackets mine).

God is telling mankind that the invisible things from the very creation of the world are clearly seen. How? . . . By the things that God has made. Therefore, if we study the world around us, we can understand the invisible world. God further states that we can even understand the Godhead (the Trinity).

Many teach that the Trinity is a mystery and cannot be understood. I don't see it that way. If God, in His Word, clearly says that we can understand the Godhead, then it must be true.

I can just imagine all the many scholars and theologians gathered together around a huge table hashing out this so-called mystery, knit-picking every little detail, until they are all so confused they don't know what to think. Then someone lowly comes along and says, "Gentlemen, if the Lord our God stated that we can understand the Godhead by studying the things He has made, then let's simply do as He tells us and we'll have the answer". Seems fair enough, no?

After studying the things God has made, what have we come up with? How obvious can it be. . . Man himself?

In Genesis 1:26 (KJV), God said:

> "Let us make man in our image, after our likeness . . ."

WOW! The answer is staring us right in the face. Now, all we have to do is believe it.

The term God can be used either singularly or in the plural. In Genesis 1:26 it is being used in the plural, as can be seen by the use of the words "us" and "our". God the Father, God the Son and God the Holy Ghost (Holy Spirit) are three distinct, individual beings with actual bodies (of a material spiritual substance that is governed by higher laws; but nonetheless real, and can be visible); and with souls (just like our souls, but greater in every respect); and with spirits, (just like the spiritual quality in every one of us). God Himself breathed His Spirit into man that he should have life. According to Genesis 2:7 it says:

> "And the Lord God formed man out of the dust of the
> ground, and breathed into his nostrils the breath of life;
> and man became a living soul".

We are made in the image of God. In Genesis 1:26 (KJV), God said:

> "Let us make man in our image, after our likeness:" not just
> in abstract terms, but in physical terms.

All throughout the Bible it tells us that God has hands, feet, arms, front side, face, head, hair, legs, wears clothes, etc. God the Father, God the Son, and God the Holy Ghost are very real, very personal beings with bodies, souls, and spirits. Their bodies might be of a different nature than our bodies, and their souls and spirits might be of higher nature, but we, as human beings, resemble God and His nature.

The Hebrew for likeness is "demooth", meaning model, shape, fashion, similitude and bodily resemblance. Therefore, if man was made in the image and likeness of God bodily, then God must have a body and an outward shape and form.

The concept of the Trinity (or "Three-in-One"), does not mean three persons in one as some try and teach. It means that God the Father, God the Son, and God the Holy Ghost are alike in body, soul and spirit; but each is individual and agrees in one: one in thought, ideals, interests, motives, and concerns, etc. It is not any different than three human beings, all joined together toward a common goal. In a way, you could look at it like man saying: 'Let us make robots in our image; after our likeness'. Man, meaning any number of men, with like goals: combining efforts to give these robots arms, legs, head and the like; and endeavoring to impart into them as many human characteristics as is possible (but man can only make a limited facsimile of himself).

Nowhere in Scripture does it deny that God is a personal being with passions; and in particular, with a body. The Bible emphatically states that God has all these qualities. Nor does the Bible state that God is intangible and immaterial. The only verse of Scripture which might imply otherwise, is John 4:24 (KJV), which states that, "God is Spirit". However, this verse in no way teaches that God is without a body. It is only because we are unaware of what spirit consists of, or what spirit is like, that men conceive God as some sort of disembodied spirit or energy source which is everywhere and in all things.

Some say that God is light and love and that you cannot see these qualities; that you can only feel them. To think that such expressions deny God a body, then we must also deny men their bodies; for the Bible makes reference to men as: "the salt of the earth" and, "the light of the world" (Matthew 5:13-16 KJV). All such statements only designate the qualities of God and in no way prove that God is without a body any more than they do men.

Spiritual substance is as realistic as material substance, except that spiritual substance is of a higher type of matter and is also governed by higher laws. Even, Paul, in Corinthians 15:42-44, speaks of human flesh-and-bone bodies as being spiritual in the resurrection and; ". . . like unto His glorious body": Christ's glorious body as in Luke 24:29 and in Philippians 3:20-21. If human bodies that become spiritualized are still material and tangible, then it makes sense that God can have a body just as real and still be a spirit being and, as the Scriptures tells us in Genesis 1:26 (KJV) . . . *we are made in the likeness of God.*

Those who claim that such figures of speech which denote that God has bodily parts, are mere human expressions trying to convey some ideas of God. However, they fail to consider the following: All figures of speech emphasize, and make as real, or perhaps more real, the ideas they express, than if literal language were used. There can be no true figure of speech to convey an idea unless the idea conveyed is real. Thus, if God's bodily parts are mere figures, then they are the true figures of the real bodily parts of God.

Now, if God is a real personal being with a spirit body, He cannot, therefore, be Omnipresent . . . as some teach; at least not omnipresent in body. What it means is that God is present in presence only, not bodily present.

God, angels and other spirit type beings travel from place to place bodily as do men. However, their presence can be any place in the universe, provided that there are other beings who have a sense of presence, and who can experience the presence of other beings; regardless of the bodily distance that exists between them. I touch on this issue in chapter sixteen, Great Mysteries Part III, in my discussion on UFO's; so I won't detail it here.

An excellent example of this is Christ, Himself, who said in Matthew, 18:20 (KJV):

> "Where two or more are gathered together in my name,
> there am I in the midst of them".

This doesn't mean that Christ is bodily present in the midst of so many gatherings; it simply means that Christ is present in His Presence (awareness), in that His presence can be felt by all free moral agents everywhere. Presence is governed only by relationship and not bodily sight. For instance: Two individuals may feel each other's presence even if they be hundreds of miles apart bodily. Presence is association and relationship, union, acquaintance, and memory. The closer two people are in their relationship one to another, the greater their presence is to one another.

This is the **key** to knowing God: Develop your awareness of God and you'll sense His presence more and more in your life. How is this done you might ask? Jesus said:

> ". . . if you know me, you know the Father who is in heaven,
> because the Father and I are one"

Jesus Christ came into the world that through Him we might get to know God; because He, Himself, is God. And we could get to know God the Father, and God the Holy Ghost, because all three are one in agreement. In other words, as you know one, you know all.

Man's capacity for presence is quite finite. God's, however, is infinite. Constantly, the presence of God is reaching out to mankind, but few men are truly cognizant of God's presence simply because men do not develop their relationship with God to the point where they can really get to know Him. Men who do not try to know God cannot, in most cases, feel His presence in their lives to any great extent. The more one thinks about God, and learns about Him, the more of His presence can be felt. That's why it is so very important to study God's Word: To get to know Him. And, He does desire that you know Him, for He has a great deal to offer you.

If men have misconstrued the quality of God's omnipresence, perhaps they have misconstrued God's omniscient quality, being all knowing; and His omnipotent quality, being all powerful.

Throughout the Bible it is made clear that God limits His knowledge where man is concerned. God's knowledge in human affairs is, for the most part, derived from messengers (angels). God's servants (the angels) assist Him in all matters and inform Him of what's going on in the universe, and then, and only then, does God take matters into His own hands.

Scriptures such as Daniel 10:13-21, 11:1, 12:1; Zechariah 1:7-11, 6:1-8; Matthew 18:10-11 and Hebrews 2:4-5, prove that He uses free moral agents (angels) to inform Him of what's going on throughout the universe.

God has stated that certain events never even came into His mind, for we read in Jeremiah 19:5 (KJV):

"They have built also the high place of Baal, to burn their sons with fire for burnt offerings unto Baal, which I commanded them not, nor spake it, neither came it into my mind".

We also find in Genesis 6:5-7 (KJV), that God did not know beforehand that mankind would become so wicked, for we read:

"And God saw that the wickedness of men was great in the earth, and that every imagination of the thoughts of his heart was only evil continually. And it repented the Lord that He had made man on the earth. And the Lord said, I will destroy man whom I have created from the face of the earth; both man, and beast, and the creeping things, and the fowls of the air; for it repented Me that I have made them".

It is obvious that if God had known beforehand that men would have become so evil, He would not have created man. It's not that God didn't realize that mankind, as free moral agents, could fall into sin; for Lucifer was a free moral agent and he certainly did sin; but God had no way of knowing beforehand to what degree any man would become sinful. God limits His omniscience by nature, or by His own will, so as to not interfere with man's freedom of choice.

There are more than 6,000 commands in the Scriptures which are designed to regulate man; over 1,000 curses and blessings made by God upon man; and over 1,500 "ifs" . . . indicating conditional circumstances to God's blessings and curses. Such commands, promises, curses and conditions, provide ample proof that God does not cause all things to happen by His own decree. It is not that God can't, it's just that He doesn't (for whatever His divine reasons might be).

These conditions set forth in the Bible prove that God does change His dealings with men as they abide by or refuse to abide by His Will. Facts such as these make it most clear that God does not know what any man will do at any given time unless He imposed Himself on man's free will . . . which He doesn't.

From the very beginning God had an eternal plan for mankind and He has the power to complete that plan. He knew that there was always the possibility that men would fall into sin, and He knew beforehand what He would do if man did fall. Nonetheless, the actual extent to which men would become sinful, He could not, or would not, know.

In your dealings with other people how often have you heard the expression: "I don't even want to know about it". Since we are made in the image and likeness of God, then perhaps, God reacts similarly.

Let me provide an example of what I mean:

Have you ever been instructed on how to do something, and in the process of being taught, you get so excited that you want to say to your instructor: "No more talk; let me just do it!" You're so anxious about doing this thing that your instructor steps aside knowing all too well that there is much more that you need to learn, but he does not wish to interfere with your excitement and your choice to get involved. What your instructor was, in fact doing, was limiting his power of control over you by his own choice in order for you to feel more at liberty to express yourself in a manner you deemed worthy. Your instructor stood by you in order to keep you from making too many mistakes; but he felt that for your excitement and benefit, he would allow you to express yourself freely. This is actually exciting for the instructor as well, for he is not certain to what extent you'll accomplish your task, but he knows that you will eventually accomplish it; because he knows you.

That's one thing I love about the Lord. As long as I don't reject Him, He lets me learn at my own pace, making mistakes along the way, and with His being very patient about it all. Every being that God created is very different and unique. God deals with every one of us individually, and with unbounded love. If we reject Him, He'll still be there for us; but He cannot help us at that point. We must come back for His help. Why? He doesn't want to disrupt our gift of "free choice".

God's omnipotent (all powerful) quality, like His other qualities, He has limited where mankind is concerned. In God's own realm He is all powerful. However, there are certain areas in which He is limited. For example: God cannot lie (Hebrews 6:17-19 KJV); God cannot deny Himself (II Timothy 2:13 KJV); God cannot have respect of persons (Romans 2:11 KJV, Colossians 3:25 KJV); God cannot save a soul apart from faith in Christ Jesus (Romans 3:25, John 3:16, Ephesians 2:8-9 KJV); God cannot curse men who meet His conditions (Mark 1:15, Luke 13:1-50 KJV); God cannot change His eternal plan (Acts 15:18, Ephesians 2:7 KJV); God cannot save rebels who reject Him (Proverbs 1:22-33, 29:1 KJV).

By His own admission God limits Himself. We cannot state factually whether God limits Himself by His choice or by His nature. Nonetheless, the above Scriptures show that when dealing with mankind, He does, without a doubt, limit Himself.

CHAPTER ELEVEN
THE GREATEST IS LOVE

GOD CREATED EVERY HUMAN being as a result of His tremendous love which He wanted to share. God could have created all of us simply as robots . . . programming every man to love Him. However, God wanted beings who would love Him as freely as He loves: That is why He created us as "free moral agents"; beings having freedom of choice. How fantastic is God's love for us? The answer is found in John 3:16 (KJV), which says:

> "For God so loved the world, that He gave His only begotten Son, that whosoever believeth in Him should not perish, but have everlasting life".

Also, in II Corinthians 5:21 (KJV), Paul tells us:

> "For He hath made Him [Jesus Christ] to be sin for us, who knew no sin; that we might be made the righteousness of God in Him". (Brackets mine).

Paul also states in Romans 5:8 (KJV):

> "But God commended His love towards us, in that, while we were yet sinners, Christ died for us".

Jesus Christ gave His life for us and did so, ". . . *while we were yet sinners*". In John 15:13 (KJV), it follows through with:

"Greater love hath no man than this, that a man lay down
his life for his friends".

Jesus Christ (as God) gave up His divine nature and in the man
Jesus, took on a fleshy nature in order to take the burden of our sins
upon Himself. Then, He allowed Himself to be crucified, so that sin
could be put to death with Him. Now that is love!

What's even more interesting to me is that John states. ". . .*that a
man lay down his life for his friends*". What John is expressing is that
Jesus Christ considers us His friends. Now tell me that the Lord our
God is not a personal God?

Jesus died for all men and not just for a select few. Through Jesus
all men can receive eternal life. Color, race, and creed, make no
difference. God loves everyone who will accept His Son. He even
loves those who haven't as yet accepted Jesus; for it is His desire to
spare all men as John 3:17 (KJV) so states:

> "For God sent not His Son into the world to condemn the
> world; but that the world through Him might be saved.
> He that believeth on Him is not condemned, but he that
> believeth not is condemned already, because he hath not
> believed in the name of the only begotten Son of God".

Take the time to study the wonders of heaven, the life around you,
the order of things, and all the fantastic beauty. Oh, there is a God
alright: a very personal and loving God!

There is an inseparable quality within all men which tells him
there is a God. Some will claim that God was created out of the
imaginations of men in order for men to have a crutch to lean on,
and to compensate for mankind's own lack. God, however, instilled
that need to enable men to recognize Him.

Remember the Scripture verse I presented in an earlier chapter, Romans 1:19 (KJV):

> "... that which may be known of God is **manifest** in them [men] ..." (Brackets and emphasis mine).

Did you catch it? The operative word is <u>manifest</u>. The very truth of God is in the makeup of every man. It is, however, our responsibility to search for that truth within ourselves. That truth can be found if one endeavors to get wisdom. Proverbs 2:4-5 (KJV), says:

> "If thou seeketh her [wisdom] as silver, and searchest for her [wisdom] as hid treasure; Then shalt thou understand the fear of the LORD, and find the knowledge of God". (Brackets mine).

The "Fear of the Lord", as so stated here, doesn't mean to literally have fear of God; for He is a loving God: but to discover the righteous aspect of God and have respect for His righteousness.

Try taking your mind off the tangible things of this world and think about the spiritual things that last forever; because your home, your car, your job, your money, and your body, will last but for a moment; not so for the things of the spirit. In Luke 23:46 Christ said (just before He died): *"Father, into thy hands I commend my Spirit"*, indicating that one's spirit lives on.

In II Corinthians 4:16-18 (KJV), Paul gives us further insight into this issue:

> "... but though our outward man perish, yet our inward man is renewed day by day. For our light affliction, which is but for a moment, worketh for us a far more exceeding and

*eternal weight of glory; While we look not at things which
are seen; but at the things which are not seen: for the things
which are seen are temporal; but the things which are not
seen are eternal".*

What Paul is confirming here is that the inward man (man's spirit)
continues to "renew" or grow even though our physical bodies die.
Also, when Paul states that, ". . . for our light affliction which is, but
for a moment . . .", he is confirming that time is non-essential in the
scheme of things (or as compared to eternity). Paul then continues
on with the words, "eternal weight of glory", in an attempt to let
mankind understand that the glory we will share in eternity, will
far exceed any of the temporary afflictions that we might experience
here on earth, and that there is no comparison as to how great our
glory will be.

Paul says that the things seen (physical world) are temporal, and the
things not seen (spiritual world) are eternal. What are the things not
seen? One thing is the glory of God Himself; we cannot experience
His Glory while we are in our physical form. Other things not seen
are all the fantastic wonders in the spiritual realm. According to the
Scriptures, we can't begin to comprehend those things which God
has in store for those that believe in His Son, as noted in Revelation
21:7 (KJV). In addition, there will be no more pain, suffering, sorrow
or tears, whatsoever, as stated in Revelation 21:4 (KJV):

*"And God shall wipe away all tears from their [the Believers,
Saints] eyes; and there shall be no more death, neither
sorrow, nor crying, neither shall there be any more pain:
for the former things are passed away".* (Brackets mine).

Jesus said in John 14:1-3, that in His Father's house there are many
mansions just waiting to be filled by Believers, for we read:

"Let not your heart be troubled: ye believe in God, believe also in Me. In my Father's house are many mansions: if it were not so, I would have told you. I go to prepare a place for you. And if I go to prepare a place for you, I will come again, and receive you unto Myself; that where I am, there you may be also".

God's Holy City is a most beautiful place. And it will, in the future, be brought from out of the North Parts (of the Universe) to be situated here on earth in Jerusalem. Read for yourself how John describes God's Holy City in Revelation chapter 21. It's way too much to include in this work, but well worth your time and effort to read, for it's absolutely wondrous.

Before closing this chapter I would like to share a beautiful essay written by a gentleman by the name of Josh Harris, who authorized this posting. This piece touched my heart and, hopefully, it will touch yours. I present to you Mr. Harris's awesome essay:

The Room

"In that place between wakefulness and dreams, I found myself in the room. There were no distinguishing features except for the one wall covered with small index card files. They were like the ones in libraries that list titles by author or subject in alphabetical order. But these files, which stretched from floor to ceiling and seemingly endless in either direction, had very different headings.

As I drew near the wall of files, the first to catch my attention was one that read "Girls I have liked". I opened it and began flipping through the cards. I quickly shut it, shocked to realize that I recognized the names written on each one. And then without being told, I knew exactly where I was.

This lifeless room with its small files was a crude catalog system of my life. Here were written the actions of my every moment, big and small, in a detail my memory couldn't match.

A sense of wonder and curiosity, coupled with horror, stirred within me as I began randomly opening the files and exploring their content. Some brought joy and sweet memories; others a sense of shame and regret so intense that I would look over my shoulder to see if anyone was watching.

A file named "Friends" was next to one marked, "Friends I have Betrayed". The titles ranged from the mundane to the outright weird. "Books I Have Read", "Lies I Have Told", "Comfort I Have Given", "Jokes I Have Laughed At". Some were almost hilarious in their exactness: "Things I Have Yelled at My Brothers". Others I couldn't laugh at: "Things I Have Done in My Anger", "Things I Have Muttered Under My Breath at My Parents". I never ceased to be surprised by the contents. Often there were many more cards than expected. Sometimes fewer than I hoped. I was overwhelmed by the sheer volume of the life I had lived.

Could it be possible that I had the time in my years to fill each of these thousands or even millions of cards? But each card confirmed this truth. Each was written in my own handwriting. Each was signed with my signature.

When I pulled out the file marked "TV Shows I Have Watched", I realized the files grew to contain their contents. The cards were packed tightly, and yet after two or three yards, I hadn't found the end of the file. I shut it, shamed, not so much by the quality of shows but more by the vast time I knew that file represented.

When I came to a file marked "Lustful Thoughts", I felt a chill run through my body. I pulled the file out only an inch, not willing to test its size, and drew out a card. I shuttered at its detailed content. I felt sick to think that such a moment had been recorded. An almost animal rage broke on me.

One thought dominated my mind: No one must ever see these cards! No one must ever see this room! I have to destroy them! In insane frenzy I yanked the file out. Its size didn't matter now. I had to empty it and burn the cards. But as I took it at one end and began pounding it on the floor, I could not dislodge a single card. I became desperate and pulled out a card, only to find it as strong as steel when I tried to tear it. Defeated and uttlerly helpless, I returned the file to its slot. Leaning my forehead against the wall, I let out a long, self-pitying sigh.

And then I saw it. The title bore "People I Have Shared the Gospel With". It was brighter than those around it, newer, almost unused. I pulled on its handle and a small box not more than three inches long fell into my hands. I could count the cards it contained on one hand. And then the tears came. I began to weep. Sobs so deep that they hurt. They started in my stomach and shook through me. I fell on my knees and cried. I cried out of shame, from the overwhelming shame of it all. The rows of file shelves swirled in my tear-filled eyes. No one must ever, ever know of this room. I must lock it up and hide the key. But then as I pushed away the tears, I saw Him.

No, please not Him. Not here. Oh, anyone but Jesus. I watched helplessly as He began to open the files and read the cards. I couldn't bear to watch His response. And in the moments I could bring myself to look at His face, I saw a sorrow deeper than my own. He seemed to intuitively go to the worst boxes. Why did He have to read every one? Finally He turned and looked at me from across the room. He looked at me with pity in His eyes. But this was a pity that didn't anger me. I dropped my head, covered my face with my hands, and began to cry again. He walked over and put His arm around me. He could have said so many things. But He didn't say a word. He just cried with me.

Then He got up and walked to the wall of files. Starting at one end of the room, He took out a file and, one by one, began to sign His name over mine on each card. "No!" I shouted rushing to Him. All I could find to say was "No, no!", as I pulled the cards from Him. His name shouldn't be on these cards. But there it was, written in red so rich, so dark, and so alive.

The name of Jesus covered mine. It was written with His blood. He gently took the card back. He smiled a sad smile and began to sign the cards. I don't think I'll ever understand how He did it so quickly, but the next instant it seemed I heard Him close the last file and walk back to my side.

He placed His hand on my shoulder and said, "It is finished".

I stood up, and He led me out of the room. There was no lock on its door. There were still cards to be written.

'For God so loved the world, that He gave His only begotten Son, that whoever believes in Him shall not perish, but have everlasting life' John 3:16'.

This, my friends, is "The Determining Factor":

No Christ, No Hope

Know Christ, Know Hope!

CHAPTER TWELVE
WHAT DO I DO NOW?

WHAT HAS BEEN PRESENTED in this work should be of great concern to every reader. It is my hope that you will take the necessary steps required to enable you to survive the trials forthcoming and to be assured of your eternal security.

And, yes, I have presented the "Good, the Bad, and the Ugly"; however, it does not have to remain "Bad or Ugly" for you. Trust in Christ Jesus and only the "Good" portion will be your inheritance.

So, you say, "What can I do?" First of all, let me encourage you to pray. Some say, "Don't you believe it; prayer doesn't work!" Nonsense! Prayer does work, and mightily so. It's prayer that Jesus encouraged. Prayer might not work the way you think it should, or in your frame of timing; but be assured, prayer works. Believe me, I know; I talked against prayer for a portion of my life and, guess what? I was wrong! God rewards those that pray with a sincere heart and who believe that their prayers are being answered: perhaps not the way you want or in the timing you deem fit; But, God does answer all prayer. The Lord is sovereign; however, He is not in absolute control, as explained in the previous chapter. God does not choose to control the actions of "free moral agents", such as we are. If He did, we wouldn't be free. There is a difference between being sovereign and being in control. God reigns over all things and He certainly has the power to see everything through as He wills. Part of that "power exertion", however, is to keep man's "free choice" intact. As a result, Satan can and does do all he can to disrupt the lives of Believers by using their gift of "free choice" against them. If we give Satan an inch into our lives, he'll grab up a mile.

Keep in mind that all the things you might pray for are not necessarily the best things for you or for those for whom you pray. Let God be the judge of what's best for you and others. Also, rest assured that no matter how awkward your prayers might seem they are a form of praise unto the Lord. The Spirit of God will take your seemingly unproductive attempts at prayer and turn them into a sweet aroma for the Lord. Remember, it's your heart's true intent and not simply what comes forth from your mouth that pleases God. Pray it, believe it, and be assured, God will handle it; in His time and in His way!

The next thing to do is to get into God's Word, the Bible. But do so with a sincere heart and with the desire to learn. It might seem confusing to start with, but if you ask God to provide you wisdom and understanding, He will . . . perhaps not all at once, for you won't necessarily be capable early on in your study to understand everything but be confident; wisdom and understanding will come. Please be patient. Start with the four Gospels of Matthew, Mark, Luke and John. I, personally, find the Gospel of John to be especially easy to follow, so you might wish to start there. The Lord will honor your effort even if you do not feel that you're receiving a great deal of enlightenment right away. He might want to "test the waters" of your heart's sincerity first; but He will take your honest effort as a sign of your willingness to change and learn.

And lastly, I highly recommend memorizing a verse from Proverbs 3:5-6 (KJV) that will bring you continued encouragement and direction:

> "Trust in the Lord with all thine heart; and lean not unto thine own understanding. In all thy ways acknowledge him, and he shall direct thy paths".

Getting involved with a sound Bible believing church and/or Bible study group is wise. You'll need the support of others who already have understanding. The Scriptures say that, we need to work out our salvation, and if you do the above, that's a great start!

I would also suggest that you watch some of the TV evangelists like: "Billy Graham", "Dr. David Jeremiah", "Dr. Charles Stanley", "Hal Lindsey", "Bayless Conley", and others. Even more so, I recommend that you secure copies of Johnathan Cahn's DVDs titled, "The Harbinger Decoded" and "The Mystery of the Shemitah Unlocked". If you watch these DVDs, I promise you, they will enlighten you beyond any other source as to what's developing worldwide and provide much needed clarity. In my opinion, these DVDs tell it all. You can secure copies from Christianbook Distributors (www. christianbook.com) for only $8.99 each, which is 40% less than most other sources. These DVDs will change the way you think!

Before closing, you need to do something. It is imperative that you surrender your heart to the Lord so that God's Spirit can work mightily on your behalf. With the utmost in sincerity and honesty, pray this simple prayer:

> Lord, I realize that I am a sinner and that I need Jesus to come into my heart. I am so very sorry for all my sins and ask for your forgiveness. I surrender everything to you: my heart, my mind, my will, and my body. Please take charge of my life, and lead me according to Your Will. I ask these things in the precious name of your Son, Jesus Christ.

If you say this prayer with a sincere heart the blood of Christ Jesus will cleanse you for all unrighteousness (sin) totally and completely. The blood of Jesus will cleanse you from your past sins, your present sins and your future sins forever. Yes, even sins you might commit in the future. How wonderful is that!

Knowing this, however, does not give you a license to sin. You have a responsibility now to try hard to avoid sinning. However, the Lord who created us knows that we are flesh and are subject to the wiles of the world, the flesh and the devil. Man could never, ever, overcome sin completely, for that would take perfection and only God is perfect. This very fact is why God the Father sent His only Son to die for you and for me . . . we simply are not perfect enough to atone for our own sins. And more importantly, God did this for us because He loves us; with a love beyond our comprehension.

When you surrender to God (as in the above prayer) you will be saved forever from the clutches of hell. If, as a believer, you fall weak and sin, you won't lose your place in God's kingdom: however, you can lose rewards that could be yours. The Bible clearly states that God has many fantastic rewards for those who trust in Him and abide by His commandments. Don't forsake those extra blessings which the Lord has in store for you. Learn to draw upon the strength of the Lord to help you overcome sin in your life.

But remember, the Bible states that God will not be mocked. What that means, in part, is that if your acceptance of His Son is not truly sincere, don't think for a moment that you're saved. An individual who thinks that he or she can rattle off the above prayer, and then continue on sinning with reckless abandon, is obviously not a saved person. One must want to overcome sin and must keep on trying their best even if that means asking God's forgiveness, "seventy times seven", as the Scriptures say. That is what repentance is all about: a sincere desire to change; to turn around; to do what is right. If you truly desire to change, then God's promises belong to you. One of those promises is that He'll never leave you or forsake you. So, be sincere and desire change!

And, remember: give thanks unto the Lord for all things, and in all things. Thank Him for your home, the food on your table, the clothes on your back, the birds of the air, the lilies in the fields, and more. Endeavor always to: "be content in whatsoever state you are in"; for there are always others who have it worse than you. Offer up all your trials, suffering, and setbacks to the Lord; for even trials are actual blessings from God. They are His means of fully maturing one's character, and developing patience; allowing you to gain wisdom. In the end, it will all be worth it!

May the Lord guide you in your journey and allow His truth to set you free!

CHAPTER THIRTEEN

GREAT MYSTERIES PART I

At this point I would like to digress from our conversation concerning prophecy and touch on issues which have perplexed many individuals. These topics are sensitive, but nonetheless, need addressing; because many have been negatively affected by such things as "Unidentified Flying Objects", "Extraterrestrials", "the Pyramids", "Ancient Artifacts", "Astronomical Discoveries", and other similar issues. These concerns are a compelling force and many are questioning their religious beliefs, their origin, and whether God even exists.

Let me start by making the following statement: 'What do we know about life and the universe?' What we have gained in knowledge these past thousands of years might seem incredible, yet, what we know and understand is but a single granule of sand, in thousands of seashores, in millenniums of time.

Where life began . . . well . . . I guess that's a mystery? Since the origin of life is a mystery, we can all go now on our separate ways and remain forever ignorant. Ok, problem solved, right? But wait! Perhaps we should go out on a limb and trust in our scientific community . . . but what do they know? They're in the same boat as the rest of humanity. Besides, it seems as though every time they come up with a theory, all of the sudden that theory is no longer valid. But wait! If the scientific community says that something is so, then it must be; because who else can we go to for the truth? I have a great idea:

How about . . . .

GOD!

Let's consider what the Bible has to say about life. In Psalms 90:2 (KJV), we read:

> "Before the mountains were brought forth, or ever thou hadst formed the earth and the world, even from everlasting to everlasting, thou art God".

Well, Lord: it certainly sounds plausible to me! You're God! Besides, what better explanation does mankind have other than, perhaps, the "Big Bang" theory? Then, of course, we need to understand how the "Big Bang" started, right Lord? The fact that it just happened doesn't cut the mustard with me? There has to be a creative force behind it. How about this: You thought it Lord, and Bang!, it happened. Now that makes some sense. But I have a question, Lord . . . Why? I guess that we have to search the Scriptures to find out that answer.

Paul says in Colossians 1:15-18 and Ephesians 1:3-11, 2:7, 3:9 (KJV), that:

> "All things were created by him, and for him . . . that in all things he might have the preeminence . . . that we should be holy and without blame before him in love that in the ages to come he might shew [show] the exceeding riches of his grace in his kindness toward us through Jesus Christ". (Brackets mine).

And, in Revelation 4:11 (KJV), we read:

> "Thou hast created all things, and for thy pleasure they are and were created".

Realizing this, let us continue onward with an open mind. Starting with Genesis 1:1 (KJV), we read:

"In the beginning God created the heavens and the earth..."

Maybe in order to satisfy the scientific community, He did it with a "Big Bang"! Why not? As the Lord thinkest . . . so shall it be. The Lord thought it, and Bang! . . . it was there! This idea alone generates a compatible quality between the Bible and science. However, we need to ask the question, "Why the earth and why man?"

It is my firm belief that Lucifer (Satan), who, according to the Bible, was the most beautiful and the wisest of all God's created beings, ruled the earth which God created in Genesis 1:1. However, so fine a being was Lucifer, that in his heart he felt that he was every bit as great as God Himself, for we read:

> *"For thou hast said in thine heart, I will ascend into heaven, I will exalt my throne above the stars of God: I will sit also upon the mount of the congregation, in the sides of the north [an area the Bible says is where the city of God is located and where God Himself resides]: I will ascend above the heights of the clouds; I will be like the Most High", Isaiah 14:13-14 (KJV) (Brackets mine).*

Lucifer must have ruled someone or somewhere or, how could he exalt his throne above the stars of God? And, we know it was the earth that he ruled, for the Bible tells us that Lucifer was cast out of heaven back to earth. Lucifer was on the earth ruling his subjects, and then he decided to ascend into heaven and exalt himself; at which point, God had him thrown out and cast back to earth, where he originally ruled.

According to the Scriptures, sin was found in Lucifer. Due to his excessive pride, it became sin, because he no longer considered the high position of God, or the "good of the universe as a whole", but himself only. During his tenure as ruler of the earth he, "weakened the nations" of the earth with his deceptiveness. We find this in Isaiah 14:1 (KJV):

> "How art thou fallen from heaven, O Lucifer, son of the morning! How art thou cut down to the ground [earth], which did weaken the nations". (Brackets mine).

Jeremiah 4:26 (KJV) states that Lucifer not only ruled nations but cities as well; which we shall see shortly.

So, what did the Almighty do because Lucifer and his subjects (both the fallen angels and physical men) rebelled? The Lord had destroyed, by flood waters, ". . . *the world that then was",* as indicated in Genesis 1:2 (KJV) below:

> "And the earth was without form and void; and darkness was upon the face of the deep. And the Spirit of God moved upon the face of the waters", (Emphasis mine).

In the Hebrew language, the phrase, "without form", is "tohu", which means: waste, desolate, confusion. The Hebrew word "void", is "bohu", which means empty, ruin or void. The entire expression, "tohu va bohu", in Hebrew, describes a chaotic type condition. God did not originally create the earth in chaos, but rather, in great splendor and glory. The intense sinfulness of all angels and men during this "pre-Adamite" civilization (by "pre-Adamite" I mean before Adam and Eve were ever created) warranted total destruction. Apparently, not one single angel or man was worth saving. Even during Noah's time, Noah and his family found enough favor in God's eyes that they were spared via the Ark. God destroyed this "pre-Adamite" civilization by means of a great flood, just as He did during Noah's time. However, after the flood of Noah, God promised never to destroy mankind by floodwaters again (Genesis 8:21-22).

Could it possibly be that Angelic creatures, as well as human beings, existed on earth prior to the creation of Adam and Eve? And, if so, is there any evidence that Lucifer ruled over these Angelic creatures and human beings in a "pre-Adamite" civilization?

To find out, why not consider what it states in Genesis 6:4 (KJV):

> "There were **giants** in the earth in those days; and also after that, when the sons of God [fallen angels] came in unto the daughters of men, and they bare children unto them, the same became mighty men which were of old, men of renown". (Emphasis and brackets mine).

It is unanimously accepted by Bible scholars that the expression, "sons of God", refers to fallen angels in this verse.

When one first reads this verse it sounds like what is being referred to as, 'in those days', means the days when David slew the giant, Goliath; I'm sure most of you are familiar with that story. However, this is not so. One must place, "in those days" in conjunction with, "and after that", in order to understand that <u>two sets of giants</u> in <u>two separate time periods</u> are to be noted. One set was in the "pre-Adamite" time period and the other set was in the time period following the flood of Noah.

There is no mention in Scripture as to what the giants were like that existed in the time period known as, *"in those days"* (the "pre-Adamite" period), but the Scriptures do give us some idea of what giants were like after the flood of Noah.

Many of these giants were fifteen feet tall and taller as described in Deuteronomy 3:11 (KJV) of the Old Testament Scriptures. The bedstead of "OG" (a giant), for example, was eighteen feet, nine inches long and over eight feet, four inches wide. That's one whopping large "Bad Boy" by anyone's standards . . . almost three times the size of a normal man today. We're looking at a giant larger than Sasquatch . . . just joking here folks . . . who believes in Bigfoot anyway for crying out loud?

There were two eruptions of fallen angels on the earth and each time they produced races of giants. The first eruption of these fallen angels occurred at the time when Lucifer and one third of the angels of heaven rebelled against God and God had them thrown out and cast down to earth. The second eruption occurred after the flood of Noah and ending during the time that David slew mean old Goliath. This is evidenced by the expression, *"There were giants in the earth in those days"* (those days meaning before the earth was flooded as in Genesis 1:2 or before Adam and Eve); *"and also after that"*, (meaning after the flood of Noah).

The "fallen angels" mated with the women of earth *". . . and bare children unto them"*, and these children grew to be giants, *". . . they became mighty men. . ."*

The purpose of these giant men was, in fact, to infiltrate the human race in order to destroy the seed of Christ Jesus. These giants proved and tested the Israelites up until the time of David when he killed Goliath, the last of the giants as previously mentioned. These giants lived mainly in the area called, "Canaan", which was the land promised to the Israelites by God. These Israelites were commanded by the Lord to destroy the giants because they were "of the house of Satan".

There are dozens of Scriptures discussing these giants in the Old Testament (way too many to list here). One of the more interesting ones is found in Numbers 13:33 (KJV), which states:

> "And there we saw the giants, the sons of Anak, which came of the giants: and we were in our own sight as grasshoppers, and so we were [like grasshoppers] in their sight". (Brackets mine).

There were many names for these giants in the Scriptures, and some are as follows: "Anakim", "Zanzumin", "Rephaim", "Horim", "Avim", "Nephthalim", etc.

What's my reasoning for presenting all this documentation about the giants? Simply this: These giants were originally angels created by God. Then, when Lucifer rebelled, he brought down, with himself, a third of all God's angels. These fallen angels could take on human form. So here you have spiritual creatures, called angels, taking on human characteristics, but in giant form. And why did they do this? They did it in order to destroy the Jewish race, because Satan knew that the seed of Abraham, Christ Jesus, would come out of the Jewish race and eventually bring down Satan and his cohorts. In other words, it was a way for Satan to thwart his own eventual destruction.

Getting back to the Lord creating the heaven and earth; it would seem only natural that God, in His infinite power and greatness, would do so in perfect beauty and splendor (Genesis 1:1). What then, is the reason for the destruction and dismal picture presented in Genesis 1:2 (KJV)?

> "And the earth was without form and void; and darkness was upon the face of the deep. And the Spirit of God moved upon the face of the waters".

After God created the heaven and the earth in tremendous beauty and splendor, and having placed the greatest of all His created angels in charge thereof, He was sinned against by Lucifer (because of his pride), as well as those angels who followed Lucifer in place of God. Therefore, God destroyed all life and vegetation on the earth by means of floodwaters (this was not the flood of Noah, however).

The reason that the earth was ". . . *without form and void . . .*" (Genesis 1:2), is because the flood that God brought down upon Lucifer and his fallen angels and the human beings of his day, covered absolutely everything. This is evident by the use of the words ". . . *upon the face of the deep . . .*" (Genesis 1:2). The deep meaning the extensive floodwaters that God caused.

I believe that a more accurate interpretation of ". . . *the Spirit of God moved upon the face of the waters . . .*" (Genesis 1:2), would be, ". . . *the Spirit of God **brooded** upon the face of the waters*". Why brooded? Because God was distraught over what He had to do: namely, destroying the earth and its people due to their sinfulness. According to the Strong's Concordance, the primary root meaning of the Hebrew word for "moved" is, in fact, "**brooded**", (Hebrew Raehaph, Raw-khaf . . . Root meaning to brood).

We must remember that sin was now formed in Lucifer. Therefore, as far as all of God's faithful angels were concerned, they did not know or understand what sin was, or what the result of sin would be if left to infiltrate all the universe throughout eternity. Possibly, because of their feeling so perplexed over God's actions toward Lucifer and the fallen angels that, God, in His loving-kindness, decided to show all His faithful angels why He was justified in doing what He did and why sin must be kept from infiltrating the entire universe throughout all eternity. As a result of this, God captivated mankind in time, allowing Satan (Lucifer) to cause men to sin, and allowing this sin to spread for a fixed period. Then, after this given time span elapsed (God's time span for mankind whereby the faithful angels will have been able to see for themselves the disastrous effects of sin), God will remove (by binding in the "Bottomless Pit", as the Bible calls it) the creator of sin (Satan Himself) for one thousand years. During this one thousand years (called the Millennial Reign of Christ) Jesus Christ will rule the earth in a manner in which it was intended to have been ruled if Adam and Eve had not fallen. In this way the faithful angels will see and appreciate how wonderfully men could have lived if sin had not entered into their lives. And, as a final show of cards, if you will, God looses Satan after one thousand years allowing him to deceive mankind once again. Those who fall into Satan's clutches at that time will, together with Satan, the Antichrist and the False Prophet, be cast into the "Lake of Fire" for all eternity.

Once Satan and his followers are forever locked up in hell, then time will be totally erased and life will continue on according to the Will of God.

You are probably thinking that this idea about God's faithful angels wanting to understand God's plan of salvation for mankind is crazy. Where do I get such nonsense? Where else but God's Word?

The Bible clearly states that the faithful angels had a desire to look into the salvation plan of God or, in other words, God's reasoning for destroying Satan and the unfaithful angels, and what measures God would utilize in rectifying (justifying) His actions. Let's take a close look at I Peter 1:10-12 (KJV) where we read the following:

> ". . . Of which salvation the prophets have inquired and searched diligently, who prophesied of the grace that should come unto you: (verse 10).
>
> Searching what, or what manner of time the Spirit of Christ which was in them did signify, when it testified beforehand

the sufferings of Christ, and the glory that should follow.
(verse 11).

Unto whom it was revealed, that not unto themselves,
but unto us they did minister the things, which are now
reported unto you by them that have preached the gospel
unto you with the Holy Ghost sent down from heaven; which
things the angels desire to look into". (verse 12).

Let's break down what is being presented here:

A.) In verse ten Peter is discussing how the prophets searched most diligently for understanding of salvation and that they were very well aware of the fact that the means of salvation was given by the grace of God.

B.) In verse eleven he talks about how the concept of salvation was also prophesied beforehand (even before the time of the prophets of Peter's day).

C.) Then in verse twelve, it states that this concept of salvation was revealed not only to them (as prophets) but also to those whom they preached the salvation message, with a direct leading from the Holy Spirit.

The idea here is that this plan of salvation was of great interest to the prophets. However, in the last part of verse twelve it states that this concept of salvation was not only of interest to the prophets, but of interest to God's faithful angels as well, for we read:

". . . which things [those things pertaining to salvation] the
angels desire to look into". (Brackets mine).

And why do you think those faithful angels desired to look into God's plan for mankind's salvation? They wanted to understand why God was justified in condemning Lucifer and those who rebelled with him. They also wanted to understand how this "sin" concept could be a destructive force that needed to be dealt with severely, totally, and completely. They wanted to see first-hand how such a problem could be dealt with effectively, yet with love, compassion and mercy (which are the attributes of God), as are His attributes of righteousness and justice. A rather complex situation, wouldn't you agree . . . but not for God!

God had planned the creation of man all along and wasn't about to change His plans because of Lucifer. God might have altered His plans to work around the Satan dilemma, but it was not outside His control. He simply had to work around the boundaries of "free will". When God created angels and humans with "free will", He also allowed for an alternative plan if any "free will agents" turned against Him, as did Lucifer.

God's purpose for creating mankind in the first place was so God could share His love and at the same time, be loved in return . . . **That's our purpose for existing.** That's why God created us with free wills, so that we could and would love Him freely. However, "free will" demands self-control and obedience. This is required in order not to disrupt the good of the universe as a whole.

Here is probably the most important lesson for us to grasp:

Our purpose for existing is to:
Love God freely, Openly and Completely.

Once we are able to accomplish this, there won't be anything that the Almighty would not do for you and for me . . . nothing!

Even in our weakened human condition, when we love someone, we desire to do wonderful things for that special individual. God can do anything, so just imagine the possibilities waiting for us in the next life. As II Corinthians 4:17 (KJV), so states:

> "For our light affliction, which is but for a moment, worketh
> for us a far more exceeding and eternal weight of glory".

Why do you think the Scriptures tell us to, *"be anxious for nothing?"* (Philippians 4:6). Because God knows what He has in store for those who love Him and we cannot attain to our full desires here on earth. Only when we meet with Him will it be so.

CHAPTER FOURTEEN
GREAT MYSTERIES PART II

DARWIN! NOW HERE IS a man who has single-handedly thrown the whole concept of salvation through Christ out the "proverbial window". And, to top that off, our society has not only allowed this ridiculous theory to become a mainstay in our lives, but has replaced the truth with the greatest lie of all times. Then we have allowed this lie to be taught in our school systems and have disallowed the truth of "creationism". At the very least, one would think that both should be taught . . . side-by-side . . . letting our hearts decide what is the truth, and what is the lie. But no, we simply go for all the lies, and all the deceptions, and force our kids to accept it. God forgive us all!

If one wishes to believe that he evolved from the lower species, then so be it. However, I would like to share something that just might awaken your genius to new heights.

Let's define a couple of words: Make (made) and Create. Webster defines them as follows:

- Make: To bring into being; specifically to form by shaping together, physically or mentally; build, construct, fabricate, cause; bring about; produce.
- Create: To cause to come into existence.

There is a fine line between these two words and many use them interchangeably. If there were not some important difference in their meanings, only one word would be needed. What then, is the actual difference? A more careful examination of their meanings would produce definitions as follows:

- Make: To bring about by fabricating from existing materials.
- Create: To bring forth out of nothing.

Now we can get into what Genesis 1:1 through 1:31 is all about. Let's analyze this chapter with a different perspective in mind. Starting in Genesis 1:1 (KJV), it states:

"In the beginning God created the heavens and the earth".

This makes sense. Whether it was with a "Big Bang" or not, God, brought into existence, from nothing, the heavens and the earth . . . He thought it, and it happened.

Then, as previously discussed, God gave the earth over to the rule of Lucifer. Lucifer, then rebels against Almighty God and, as a result, God destroyed the earth that then was by flood waters as indicated in Genesis 1:2 (KJV):

"And the earth was without form, and void; and darkness was upon the face of the deep. And the Spirit of God moved [**brooded**] *upon the face of the waters"* (Brackets and emphasis mine).

From Genesis 1:3 through Genesis 1:31 we see God either **"making"** or *"Having the earth bring forth its seed"*. This leaves the reader with the idea that what God is doing is "renovating", (fabricating from existing materials that which was brought forth in Genesis 1:1 where it states that, "and God created"). Then in verse 21, a different term is used . . . **created**. Here it says, *"And God underline{created} great whales, and every living creature that moveth . . ."*.

Backing up a verse we find that, Moses, the accepted writer of Genesis, describes what God wanted to do:

> "And God said, let the waters bring forth abundantly the
> moving creature that hath life, and the fowl that may fly
> above the earth in the open firmament of heaven".

While in verse 21 God commands it to be so, for it says: *"And God created"*.

In verse 25 where the word "made" is used once again, it had been used with the concept of reconfirming what God had already completed. This is proved by the fact that in verse 21 it emphatically states*: "God created every living creature . . ."*. Then in verse 27 it states that:

> "God created man in his own image, and in the image of
> God created He him; male and female created He them".

After the "pre-Adamite" flood (the flood before Adam and Eve . . . not the flood of Noah), certain things God had previously created were totally wiped off the face of the earth, such as man. But please keep in mind, however, that certain life forms, such as whales and fish (aquatic creatures) didn't exist in the beginning because as you'll soon discover, there were no seas, lakes or oceans "In the beginning . . .". Therefore, when God renovated the earth after the "pre-Adamite" flood, He not only had to create man once again, but now, since there was water left on the earth from the flood, He decided to create whales and aquatic life as well.

After the flood Noah experienced, God did not have to "re-create" certain things because they <u>were not</u> totally wiped out of existence; so all He did was renovate things such as: plants, trees, mountains, etc. However, after the "pre-Adamite" flood, certain life forms such as man and whales had to be created. After the flood of Noah's time, God did not have to create new life forms because most were saved via the "Ark", except for certain Aquatic life that never did exist previously.

The act of God creating the *"heaven and the earth"* of Genesis 1:1 was a separate act from the destruction of the earth as in Genesis 1:2. This is proved by the use of the word "**and**". In the first two chapters of Genesis the word "and" is used well over one hundred times to separate certain acts of God. These acts of God were independent of each other. The "and" of verse two proves that the act of destroying, *"the earth that then was"*, was entirely independent of the act of creating the earth in verse one.

To further substantiate this point, I wish to share the following:

In Genesis 1:10 (KJV), the earth is called "dry land" which means Genesis 1:1 could read, *"In the beginning God created the heaven and the dry land"*. Since the earth was created dry (not overflowing with deep water as in Genesis 1:2), it opens the door of possibility that the earth was inhabited; and that the waters of Genesis 1:2 (or flood), was a curse and not a creative act.

According to Psalm 136:6 (KJV), the earth was originally created dry and "stretched above the waters"; not the waters stretched upon the earth. This presupposes a "pre-Adamite" race whose sin brought such a curse; just like the curse that the flood brought upon the people living during the time of Noah, due to their wickedness.

In Genesis 2:5-6 (KJV), it states:

> ". . . for the LORD God had not caused it to rain upon the earth, and there was no man to till the ground. But there

*went up a mist from the earth, and watered the whole face
of the ground".*

These verses are evidence that there were no bodies of water upon
the earth at this time but, rather, dry ground. A mist that came up
from under the ground provided all necessary water.

As for the words, *". . . and there was no man to till the ground . . .",*
this doesn't mean there were no men at this time. It is presented
in the sense that there was no need for men to till the ground
because, like during the time of Adam and Eve, they were provided
all necessary food without having to till the ground, plant seeds and
then harvest the food.

In Genesis 1:2 the earth is not only flooded with water but covered
in total darkness; the sun, moon, and stars having withdrawn
their light, causing all life on earth to be totally destroyed. This
presupposes a "pre-Adamite" world of birds, animals, vegetation
and man, because the only purpose for light is for plant growth and
to provide mankind with sight and warmth. What purpose would
there be for light if there were no plants, vegetation, animals and
man to utilize it?

My point here is to show that it was highly probable and very
possible that a race of men existed on the earth prior to the creation
of Adam and Eve. If Lucifer ruled the earth (as the Bible so states),
he must have had subjects to rule. Isaiah 14:12 (KJV), says:

> "How art thou fallen from heaven, O Lucifer, son of the
> morning! How art thou cut down to the ground, which didst
> weaken the nations!" (Emphasis mine).

There must have been, therefore, nations of people for Lucifer to rule
over, for how could he "weaken the nations"?

Lucifer, because of his terrible pride, turned the nations of the earth against God and, God was forced, out of supreme justice, to destroy all that then was.

To expound on this point further, let's turn to Jeremiah 4:23-26 KJV, which states:

> "I beheld the earth, and lo, it was without form, and void; and the heavens, and they had no light. I beheld the mountains, and, lo, they trembled, and all the hills moved lightly. I beheld, and, lo, there was no **man** and all the birds of the heavens were fled. I beheld, and, lo, the fruitful place was a wilderness, and all the **cities** thereof were broken down at the presence of the Lord, and His fierce anger". (Bold emphasis mine).

Jeremiah emphatically states that both **man** and **cities** were destroyed because of the Lord's *"fierce anger"*. Therefore, Lucifer must have ruled **mortal men, cities and nations**.

One might wish to question whether or not this describes a "pre-Adamite" time when Lucifer ruled men, cities and nations. It is my firm belief that it does.

First of all, the only time the Bible records the earth as being without form and void, is in Genesis 1:2, which occurred before the six days of creation (renovation) starting in Genesis 1:3. Also, the only time that the Bible records the sun, moon and stars not giving their light was prior to the six days of creation (or renovation) starting in Genesis 1:3 and, again, during the Tribulation period of the end times. Since the Tribulation is an event yet future it could not possibly refer to this period, thus, leaving it to occur prior to the six days of creation as noted in Genesis 1:3-31, and the advent of Adam and Eve. Jeremiah 4:23-26 is not a prophecy and, therefore, could not be discussing an event yet future.

These verses cannot depict the flood of Noah, for Noah and his family, along with animals and birds, were obviously saved via the Ark in order to continue their species. Yet, Jeremiah clearly states in verse 25, that: "*. . . there was **no man** and **all the birds of the heaven fled**"*. The expression, ". . . the birds of the heaven fled", is simply another way of expressing that all the birds disappeared.

In Genesis 1:28 (KJV), God commanded Adam and Eve to replenish the earth, for we read:

> "*And God blessed them, and God said unto them, Be fruitful, and multiply, and **replenish** the earth . . .*" (Bold emphasis mine).

Now let me ask you: **"How can something be replenished that did not previously exist?"** Not all Bibles use the word "replenish". In fact, as far as I know, only the original 1611 version of the King James Bible (the Bible that scholars refer to) uses the term "replenish". Most of the modern Bibles use the term "to fill"; and I, personally, feel that is erroneous.

Adam and Eve were commanded by the Lord to establish another race of mortal men that were to replace the race which, I firmly believe, God had previously destroyed in Genesis 1:2.

The Hebrew word for replenish is ma'le (maw-lay). And, yes, it is true that the primary root meaning is to "fill" or be "full of". However, it is also defined as "replenish".

Some scholars interpret ma'le as "fill", rather than replenish, because the primary root meaning is "to fill". This, of course, could change the concept of "replenishing" or putting back what was originally there, into filling, but not necessarily something of a like nature and quality. So who's correct?

In my discussion of Genesis 1:2 concerning the meaning of "moved" as brooded, I did so based on the fact that the root meaning of the word was "brooded". One could say, then, that the same principle should apply when deciding the meaning of "replenish" in Genesis 1:28.

That's a reasonable and fair approach and one would not necessarily be in error taking such an approach. However, the actual context of the verses where a word is used is also very important in determining an exact meaning. Let's consider then the whole verse and you can determine for yourself which is correct.

God said, ". . . *Be fruitful, and multiply, and replenish the earth . . .*". If we replaced the word "replenish" with the word "fill", the verse would then read: ". . . Be fruitful, and multiply, and fill the earth . . .". To say "multiply" and "fill" in the same verse seems redundant. Although "multiply" and "fill" have somewhat different meanings, they also have somewhat of the same meaning; and that meaning is, to increase! However, if we were to leave the verse in its original form, the word "multiply" would mean to increase and the word "replenish" would mean to put back what was originally there. It's no different than asking someone to multiply (increase) that which was originally. This combination of words does seem, to me anyway, a more correct way to express what God had intended for Adam and Eve to do. This, of course, is open to each and everyone's own interpretation.

In a final effort to establish firm ground for this belief in the existence of a "pre-Adamite" race of men, I wish to give you the following verses:

"For this they willingly are ignorant of, that by the Word of God the heavens were of old [Genesis 1:1], and the earth standing out of the water [Genesis 1:1] and in the water [Genesis 1:2]. Whereby the earth that then was [Genesis 1:1], being overflowed with water, **perished** [Genesis 1:2]: But the heavens and the earth, which are now [Genesis 1:3-31], by the same word are kept in store, reserved unto fire against the day of judgment and perdition of ungodly men". II Peter 3:5-7. (Bold emphasis and brackets mine).

The word **perished** describes a destructive act. The destructive act was the flooding of the "pre-Adamite" race of angels, men and animals that existed prior to the earth being renovated in Genesis 1:3-31. As I mentioned before about the word "moved" as used in Genesis 1:2, being more accurately interpreted as "brooded" (because God was distraught over having had to destroy the race that then existed because of their wickedness); "brooded" is further substantiated by the use of the word "**perished**". God would not "brood" over simply causing water to form, but He certainly could "brood" over His creating a flood to cause something, or someone, to perish. At least, as human beings, I think most of us would probably react that way, and we certainly are made unto God's likeness.

I mentioned earlier of a period which is yet future referred to as the Millennium (or one thousand year reign of Christ). It is my firm belief that in God's plan to show His faithful subjects (angelic beings) why He was justified in condemning Lucifer, the Lord had to illustrate that rulership under God is the only way that existence, which is beneficial for the good of the entire universe, can be realized. Lucifer ruled men to start with and failed miserably. The result of his failure is being experienced by us today. However, Jesus Christ must complete His Father's plan for justification by doing that which was commanded of Lucifer before Adam's day. And what Lucifer should have done, but didn't, was to rule the earth in love and place God above all. When Christ returns to set up His kingdom during the Millennium, He will rule the earth in total love and righteousness.

The bottom line is that the above discourse shows evolution to be a ridiculous theory which in basis says: "nothing, working on nothing, through nothing, for nothing . . . begat everything".

Evolution endeavors to nullify the truth of the Biblical account of creationism. The concept of nothing, acting upon nothing, by nothing, to evolve everything, is substituted for the creative power of a very personal and loving God who has provided mankind with evidence of His very Being. Evolution degrades man and insults God, who said, *"Let us make man in our image"*. It's the same as saying that man is a monkey and, God, a monkey's uncle! Evolution certainly does deny Christ's atonement; because if there is no fall of mankind, there can be no sin for which to atone. Evolution denies the validity of God's Word and the power thereof.

In short, evolution denies God, man, salvation and life after death. It is a theory which, if believed in whole or in part, will place the believer in Satan's clutches.

To summarize, let me recap an article written by George Plagenz, from the March 14, 1981 edition of the Cleveland Press:

> "The fact that most school children are exposed to nothing but a "Godless" neo-Darwinian philosophy regarding the origin of the universe had led some parents to conclude that this is partly responsible for the students "deadened spiritual lives", which have produced, in turn, many of the social evils now plaguing society.

Time magazine this week quotes a Georgia judge as saying: "This monkey mythology of Darwin is the cause of permissiveness, promiscuity, pills, prophylactics, perversions, pregnancies, abortions, pornography, pollution, poisoning, and proliferation of crimes of all types.

The sudden appearance in the fossil record of complex animals disproves the theory of progressive evolution, 'says a zoologist at the University of Southern California'. 'If progressive evolution were a fact, the fossil record should reveal a continuous graduation from simple to complex. But it doesn't. On the basis of what is actually found in the earth, the theory of a sudden creative act fits best."

If, as illustrated, a "pre-Adamite" race of men existed prior to Adam and Eve, then the evolution theory simply falls apart.

One additional thought. Some individuals might question the last portion of the above Scripture verse, II Peter 3:5-7 which states:

"But the heavens and the earth, which are now [Genesis 1:3-31], by the same word are kept in store, reserved unto fire against the day of judgment and perdition of ungodly men".

Some claim that if the heavens and earth which are now, are being kept in store and reserved unto fire, where does the flood of Noah come into play? God did promise Noah He would never destroy the earth with flood waters ever again. However, one needs to consider at what point ". . . the heavens and the earth, which are now . . ." come into play. The answer is: after the flood of Noah's time. This does open the door allowing for the earth to be "reserved unto fire" in the future.

CHAPTER FIFTEEN
GREAT MYSTERIES PART III

We now come to the mystery of UFOs and USOs (Unidentified Submerged Objects). So prepare yourself, because I feel they are not what most have been led to believe.

UFOs and USOs have played and will continue to play an important role in Biblical prophecy and the fulfillment of God's plan for mankind. I believe that UFOs and USOs are both Angelic, as well as demonic in nature, and come from a fourth dimension (possibly even a greater dimension) and <u>are not all "extraterrestrial"</u> in form. I say this because Angelic beings can be from anywhere in the universe, but demonic beings cannot (which I hope to prove shortly).

The Bible makes it quite plain and clear that we are definitely being fought over by very powerful demonic spiritual forces. On the one side, you have Satan and his demonic forces, and on the other side you have the Lord God Almighty and His Angelic forces.

When God cast Lucifer and his fallen angels out of heaven, that's exactly what the Lord did. Lucifer's domain (according to Scripture) is the earth and the heavens immediately surrounding the earth. Godly Angelic beings, however, rule the entire universe and beyond.

As life goes on in the physical world, so does life go on in the supernatural (spiritual) world. The physical world and the supernatural world coexist. The Scriptures tell us that, for in I Corinthians 13:12 (KJV), it says:

> "For now we see through a glass darkly; but then face to
> face: now I know in part; but then shall I know even as also
> I am known".

Let me help clarify this verse. Did you ever look through a glass window at night when there were no lights shining anywhere? Perhaps, and just for example; you stayed in a cabin in the woods on a fishing trip, a hunting trip, or just to be with your spouse in order to get away from the hustle-bustle of life. As you looked out the cabin window you couldn't really see anything because of the intense darkness; yet, you knew that much was going on outside that you simply could not see. There were animals of various types on the prowl and birds, like owls, perched on the limbs of trees waiting to pounce down on some unsuspecting creatures. That is what Paul is talking about in the above verse when he refers to: "a glass darkly". You can't see what's really out there, but you know something is taking place. Well, in Ephesians 6:12 (KJV), it tells us what's going on, for we read:

> "For we wrestle not against flesh and blood, but against
> principalities, against powers, against the rulers of darkness
> of this world".

WOW! Powerful stuff, isn't it? The battles that are being waged in the supernatural realm have been taking place ever since mankind entered the scene (perhaps even longer). The battles are, to a great extent, over man himself.

In the very distant past when Lucifer was given the earth, his throne, and power to rule (both angels and men) everything went smoothly at first. Then something happened. Satan began to think bad thoughts. You know, such things as: "I'm just as beautiful as God"; or, "I'm just as wise as He is"; or, My power is just as strong as the Lord's power", etc. Lucifer's pride got the better of Him and he attempted to elevate himself to the point of thinking he could be equal to, or better than, God Almighty. Well, we know from Scripture that that didn't sit well with the Lord, so the Lord cast Lucifer out of heaven and back down to earth. However, in the process, Lucifer convinced a third of all the angels in heaven to rebel against God and follow him.

To establish a clearer picture of what transpired, think of this following scenario:

According to the Bible all those persons who have accepted Jesus Christ prior to the Tribulation will receive glorified bodies (for one cannot be raptured without first receiving a glorified body). Also, all those who enter into the Tribulation, and then later accept Christ, because they realized the error of their ways, and who are then raptured, will also receive glorified bodies; and only those with glorified bodies can reign with Christ. (Reference I Corth. 15:51-54).

> "Blessed and holy is he that hath part in the first resurrection [the Rapture]: on such the second death hath no power [because of their glorified bodies], but they [the believers] shall be priests of God and of Christ, and shall reign with him a thousand years". Revelation 20:6 KJV (Brackets mine).

Jesus Christ, along with His Saints, as well as the martyred Tribulation Saints, will have immortal bodies (glorified, spiritual bodies): but any people who survive the Tribulation, without experiencing physical death, will retain their mortal, physical bodies (just like you and I have right now). To prove that the martyred Tribulation Saints will rule during the Millennium is shown in Revelation 20:4 (KJV), which states:

> "And I [John] saw thrones, and they that sat upon them: and I saw the souls of them that were beheaded for the

witness of Jesus, and for the word of God, and which had
not worshipped the beast [Antichrist], neither his image,
neither had received his mark upon their foreheads, or in
their hands; and they [the martyred Tribulation Saints)
lived and reigned with Christ a thousand years".

Those who come through the Tribulation alive do not receive glorified bodies as do the souls who are martyred; they live in physical bodies during the Millennial Reign of Christ Jesus.

So, just as Christ will rule from His throne here on earth in His spiritual, glorified body, so did Lucifer in the distant past. Also, just as the Saints of the Lord (the Raptured Believers) will rule with Him in their glorified, spiritual bodies, so did the fallen angels in the distant past rule men. And then, just like there will be natural human beings living during the Millennium, so also were there natural human beings living in the distant past (the "pre-Adamite" past) as we showed in Part One of Great Mysteries.

Satan tries to duplicate everything God does. For example: There is God the Father, God the Son, and God the Holy Ghost. Satan has his own trinity: Satan himself, the Antichrist, and the False Prophet. Also, Christ was wounded to death on the cross and Antichrist is wounded to death during the Great Tribulation. This is so proven in Revelation 13:3 (KJV):

"And 1 [John] saw one of the heads [the head of the beast
creature] as it were wounded to death; and his deadly
wound was healed: and all the world wondered after the
beast [Antichrist]". (Brackets mine).

And, as Jesus Christ rose from the dead, so will Antichrist (as shown in Revelation 13:3 above). Throughout Scripture it teaches that

Satan will endeavor to duplicate all that God puts into motion; and why not? If it works for God, why not for Satan. However, Satan won't succeed in the end!

Some might question whether or not Revelation 13:3 is talking about the Antichrist, or about the "Creature Beast"; which is representative of the last world empire (the sixth empire as previously discussed), in the chapter on, "The Last World Empire". This could possibly be so (but only in part). Here's why:

After Antichrist breaks the covenant (treaty) with Israel, and the ten kings from the ten-nation Last World Empire give over their power to Antichrist, he then becomes the sole ruler and establishes his own short-lived, self-ruling kingdom (or the sixth empire). As a result, the "Beast Creature" of Revelation 13:3 (KJV) could represent the death of the ten-nation confederacy which is brought back to life once again when Antichrist's self-ruling sixth empire is established.

The problem I see with this interpretation is that in Revelation 13:5 (KJV), it states:

> "And there was given unto him a mouth speaking great things and blasphemies; and power was given unto him to continue forty and two months [or three and one half years]". (Brackets and emphasis mine).

I can't visualize how an empire can have, *"a mouth speaking great things and blasphemies. . .".*

Perhaps the idea of, ". . . a mouth speaking great things . . ." is a metaphor for a nation speaking great things; but I really don't think so; although it is possible. Only time will tell.

Personally, I believe Revelation 13:3 is referring to both the Antichrist and the "Creature Beast" (sixth kingdom) jointly. Since Antichrist does, in fact, constitute the sixth kingdom, it is he who is wounded to death and revived.

I truly believe that Antichrist will be killed and brought back to life through the incarnation of Satan, while at the same time, the ten-nation empire (now the sixth empire) will become dead, in that its leaders surrender their power to Antichrist and a new kingdom is formed (the sixth kingdom). No matter which might be the case, it does not change the structure of the prophecy and its fulfillment.

You might find it interesting that this "Last World Empire" constitutes the "sixth empire", and that Christ's Millennial Empire constitutes a "seventh empire". In the sixth chapter, "Mathematics in Scripture", we learned that man's number is "6" and that God's number for perfection is "7". In other words, the final empire, (Christ's Millennial empire), will be a perfect empire because it'll be ruled by God. The "Last World Empire", that gets completely destroyed, is ruled by men and whose number is six. This correlates with the number "10", which is the number of worldly completion; and the final destruction of the Last World Empire will, indeed, bring finality to mankind's rule. Oh how God's Word manifests itself so uniquely!

Getting back to our discussion about UFOs and USOs, one can see how spirit beings can and do take on physical form. When the "sons of God" (the fallen angels), came in unto the daughters of men, and they bore children unto them, that is just one example (Genesis 6:4). We also know from Scripture that demons can infiltrate human beings and animals (called demonic possession).

From a brighter side, we know that Jesus Himself, after He arose from the dead took on a glorified, spiritual body which could be seen, touched, and consume food, as well as, walk through doors. Also, the two men clothed in white at the burial tomb of Jesus were angels that looked like normal men, as did the two angels who were sent to destroy Sodom and Gomorrah. This provides added proof that angels, whether Holy or demonic, can and do take on physical form.

The supernatural forces of good and evil have been, and are, constantly warring with each other. Even when Daniel did pray for understanding concerning a vision he was given, the answer to his prayer was delayed, because Satanic forces kept the messenger of God (Gabriel) from reaching Daniel with the answer; for we read in Daniel 10:12-14 (KJV):

> "Then said he [the angel] unto me, Fear not, Daniel: for from the first day that thou dist set thine heart to understand, and to chasten thyself before thy God, thy words were heard, and I am come for thy words.
>
> But the prince of the king of Persia [a Satanic angel] withstood me one and twenty days [three weeks]: but, lo, Michael [the Great Archangel], one of the chief princes [angel of God], came to help me; and I remained there with the king of Persia.
>
> Now I am come to make thee understand what shall befall thy people in the latter days: for yet the vision is for many days". (Brackets mine).

Here we can see a messenger from God (the angel Gabriel), being detained for three weeks by a fierce adversary (a Satanic angel), until Michael, God's Archangel, came to Gabriel's aid.

God employs His faithful angels to carry out His plans and to protect His people. All throughout the Old Testament Scriptures men like Joshua, Ahab, Gideon, Hezekiah and others called upon God to help them overcome their enemies. God did hear their prayers and miraculously their enemies were, indeed, overcome . . . though the odds were heavily against them. Even the great Assyrian army of 185,000 soldiers was totally destroyed in one day by the single intervention of one of God's holy angels. We read in Isaiah 37:36 (KJV) (also referenced in II Kings 19:35):

> *"Then the angel of the LORD went forth, and smote in the camp of the Assyrians a hundred and fourscore and five thousand* [185,000]: *and when they arose early in the morning, behold, they were all dead corpses".* . . (Brackets mine).

Many such victories were the result of strange occurrences which, we today, refer to as UFOs.

I am sure that many of you who read these pages have probably never realized how the Israel of today has been able to be so victorious over forces far superior to her own. You read and hear about their successes all the time in the newspapers and on TV. Many a nation has wondered in awe as to how Israel has been able to win over the far superior forces of so many of her enemies.

Consider the following article by the director of the Twentieth Century UFO Bureau, Robert Barry, who wrote in the Christian Beacon:

> *"During the Six-Day War, an armada of brilliant wheel-shaped objects flew over the Sinai Peninsula during the battle between the Israelis and Arabs. Egyptian tanks,*

> supplied by the Soviet Union, and other military vehicles were destroyed by objects through fire power as they flew over.
>
> A vision of onrushing Israeli soldiers was seen by five thousand Egyptian soldiers. They saw thousands and thousands of Jews rushing toward them in battle array, coupled with the sound of hundreds of military vehicles. To fight would have been sheer death, they thought, so they threw up their hands and surrendered without a battle".

I was in my early twenties when this happened and I can recall quite vividly how all the news reporters were amazed at the outcome and how totally confused and surprised the Egyptians were; especially the Egyptian soldiers who were interviewed: for the fear and frustration shown on the faces of the soldiers after what they had experienced, was simply unbelievable. It has left its mark on my mind ever since.

Just recently, I saw a program on the History Channel (I believe it was that channel), where they showed pictures of those Egyptian soldiers shortly after the war ended. These soldiers still showed fear in their eyes even days afterwards. The reporters who were doing the interviews, recorded what these soldiers were saying concerning what had just transpired: They said that they saw strange aerial objects of unknown origin fire down on their military vehicles from above. They explained how frightened they were of the great number of Israeli soldiers which they never knew the Israel army had in their service (yet, the Israeli's didn't have a large army). The Egyptian soldiers also claimed that they felt that it was useless to continue the battle and that's why they surrendered without fighting. Well, **Something mighty unusual and powerful had to have occurred for such a strong military force to simply give up without a fight!**

Barry previously reported in other articles of increased UFO activity during all four wars in occupied Israel: 1948, 1956, 1967, and 1973; and claimed that these UFOs have helped Israel to win victory upon victory over the far superior forces of the Arabs.

In Ezekiel 1:16 (KJV), he describes a strange sight which he had experienced:

> "The appearance of the wheels and their work was like unto the colour of a beryl: and they four had one likeness: and their appearance and their work was as it were a wheel in the middle of a wheel".

Then is verses 18 and 19 he continues with:

> "As for their rings, they were so high that they were dreadful; and their rings were full of eyes round about them four. And when the living creatures went, the wheels went by them: and when the living creatures were lifted up from the earth, the wheels were lifted up".

Ezekiel is describing these four strange creatures (all four were God's angels called Cherubims), apparently within an object the color of a beryl stone. A beryl stone is a silicate of beryllium and aluminum, of great hardness occurring in green, bluish green, yellow, pink or white hexagonal prisms. It is rather interesting that Ezekiel chose this particular stone in order to express what he had witnessed, not only because of the shape, but the color. Beryl has a variety of colors associated with it, so maybe, Ezekiel was trying to say that it pulsated with various colors.

Ezekiel also talks about a wheel within a wheel, which was, perhaps, his way of indicating that this craft had an inner and outer disk shape with the inner disk forming a control center. He also mentions rings with eyes. Perhaps the edge of the rings (the wheels) had lights. He talks about the wheels and the creatures lifting up as though they (the creatures, Cherubim) were themselves being lifted upward in this circular shaped object. Even Robert Barry described the objects that flew over the battlefield during the Six-Day war as being "Wheel-Shaped".

It is a recorded fact that during all the Middle East confrontations, increased sightings of UFOs were definitely confirmed. It is my understanding that even the Israeli military has photographs of all these UFOs in their archives, but since they are classified, they won't release them to the public.

Why all the hush-hush concerning these UFOs? I truly believe that it is extremely important for one reason in particular . . . "The Rapture"!

We discussed the Rapture in chapter 7. Briefly, again, it is the event whereby those who believe in Christ Jesus as their Lord and Savior, will be removed from the face of earth just prior to the Tribulation period. All true Believers will be translated from their physical bodies to glorified, spiritual bodies in a moment, in an instant of time. I believe that UFOs will play an important role in this major event.

When Daniel was told to ". . . *shut up the words, and seal the book, even to the time of the end; many shall run to and fro, and knowledge shall be increased . . .*"; this is one such example of the knowledge being afforded people during the last days: for today we can clearly understand the concept of teleportation as being a reality. And, in my mind, the idea of the "Rapture" sure sounds like teleportation to me! How about you? Is that too much for one to accept? I don't think so!

One of the first things that probably popped into your mind is, "If millions of Christians suddenly disappear, how will the leaders of the world (and in particular, Antichrist) explain the phenomenon to those left behind?"

In this age of "Close Encounters of the Third Kind", "Star Trek", "Star Wars", and "Ancient Aliens", and the like, the concept of teleportation or dematerialization of matter is not at all strange or unusual to us. In "Star Trek", for example, the captain and his crew members are continually being translated from the ship to a planet in a unit called a "transporter". With numerous UFO sightings being reported almost daily, combined with the imagination of movie producers, couldn't it be feasible for Antichrist to make a public broadcast to the people of earth that for years governments around the world have had contact with extraterrestrial life and that the sudden disappearance of certain people is the result of this contact. He might further explain that the "Christian Element" was the deteriorating factor in society and, therefore, had to be removed to some distant planet where they could start their own colonies ruled by their own philosophies.

Just think about it; for in I Corinthians 15:51-52 (KJV), Paul tells us:

> "Behold, I shew [show] you a mystery: we [Believers] shall not all sleep [die], but we [Believers] shall be changed, in a moment, in the twinkling of an eye . . ."

I hope that I have proven to your satisfaction that God does, indeed, have a body (spiritual body); that He is a very personal and loving God and that He employs His angels to carry out His will and plan for mankind. I pray that you can relate to the fact that God's angels do have the capacity for travelling the expanse of the universe and beyond in very sophisticated spacecraft. I pray, also, that you can now see through all the deceptions and misguided information that our media puts out and you can realize that the phenomenon of UFOs and USOs is very real; but not because they are extraterrestrials from some other far away galaxy; but rather, from a fourth dimension (or possibly from some greater dimensions that may exist).

Satan and his fellow demons can traverse the heavens just like God and His angels can. The only difference is that Satan and his forces are restricted to the earth and the near heavens. They cannot traverse the entire universe as can God and His angels.

Endeavor to understand that all the supernatural forces which we cannot see are in constant battle, and only when God so determines, will He bring everything to an end; so that the standards of Almighty God will be upheld for all eternity. Evil will then be forever displaced, and righteousness will reign supreme.

Revelation 21:2 (KJV) describes how the "Holy City of God" will be brought down from out of heaven to earth:

> "And 1 John saw the holy city, new Jerusalem, coming down from God out of heaven, prepared as a bride for her husband".

This Holy City is no small place either; for in Revelation 21:16 (KJV) an angel of the Lord is told to measure the city:

> "And the city lieth foursquare, and the length is as large as the breadth: and he [the angel] measured the city with the reed, twelve thousand furlongs [1,500 miles]. The length and breadth and the height of it are equal". (Brackets mine).

That's one huge spacecraft. Can anyone imagine the size of such a city?. . . fifteen hundred miles long, fifteen hundred miles wide, and fifteen hundred miles high. I'd like to know what kind of power plant is in that city! Gee-gosh, we all know . . . The Power of Almighty God!

SPECIAL NOTE

If you're feeling that what has been presented within these pages is too far-fetched for anyone to believe, then please consider the following:

There is an organization called "CERN" which, together with some 15 to 20 countries is involved in a project to discover how life itself came into existence.

This organization has constructed a seventeen mile long underground tunnel at the Southern France-Swiss border called the "Hadron Particle Collider". The purpose of this "Particle Collider" is to accelerate proton particles to near the speed of light. This project is the most powerful experiment ever placed in motion.

Scientists around the world want to know about the nature of creation itself, so they're attempting to "burst" subatomic particles in order to learn about "Gravitons". Gravitons are weak particles that dilute the strength of gravity, therefore allowing them to escape into other dimensions. Scientists believe that these "Gravitons" are escaping into a parallel reality which is creating a passageway (doorway) to other dimensions.

Sergio Bertolucci, science director at CERN, stated in a public interview that we are going to open a doorway at CERN where we can send something through it or receive something from it.

CERN is searching for what are called "Gluons" or "overlaying of sound waves". Particle scientists cannot understand why we, as humans, simply don't fly apart. We are almost entirely motion;

meaning our makeup consists entirely of protons, neutrons, and spinning electrons . . . we're actually in constant movement!

"Gluons" are extremely important. Gluons are the overlaying of sound waves, and are what holds everything together.

In Genesis 1:3 God said, "Let there be light", and then there was light! God SPOKE! God emits sound waves! God calls forth into "somethingness", out of "nothingness"; atomic constructs, if you will; and as a result, creates all things.

Throughout Scripture, not only God speaks out loud, but commands the prophets, the teachers, and His followers to speak out loud and publically. Why? Because doing so makes things come about (happen), particularly in the spiritual realm. What we speak enters into the spiritual realm where all things become real. We do not always recognize this truth in our physical world, but it says volumes in the spiritual realm.

This might be difficult for many to comprehend, but the scientific community is more convinced than ever before that "We Are Wrong" and that there is a creative force behind all things. The Scriptures call this creative force, "GOD". Many individuals will call it a "disembodied energy source". For myself, I'll go with what the Bible says: "In the beginning, GOD . . ."!

Why do you think the Scriptures say that God holds His Word above Himself? Because His Word brings all things into being!

In closing, let me remind you that:

The Determining Factor is:

No Christ, No Hope!

Know Christ, Know Hope!

My prayers go with you!

PLEASE RESPOND IF YOU WOULD

I would love to hear from you if this work has been inspiring and has opened your eyes as to Christ Jesus' love for you and the hope you have in Him.

Email me at <u>buckyrcb@christianman.com</u> if you would like to share how this work has changed your life . . . it sure would be appreciated.

Any testimonial you might provide would be beneficial in encouraging others.

Thank you in advance!

BIBLIOGRAPHY

Allen, Charles L., **All Things are Possible Through Prayer** (Fleming H. Revell Co., 1974).

Benson, Clarence H., and D. Litt, **The Triune God** (ETTA, 1973).

Berry, Lester V., **Biblical Quotations,** (Doubleday & Company, Inc., 1968).

Berry, George Richer, Ph.D., **The Interlinear Greek-English New Testament Lexicon** (Zondervan Publishing, 1974).

Bridges, Jerry, **Transforming Grace-Living Confidently in God's Unfailing Love** (Navpress, 1991).

Bryant, T. Alton, **The New Compact Bible Dictionary** (Zondervan Publishing, 1972).

Cantelon, Willard, **The Day the Dollar Dies** (Logos International, 1973).

Cho, Dr. Paul Yonggi, **The Fouth Dimension** (Logos Intemational, 1979).

Collins, Larry and Dominique LaPierre, **O'Jerusalem** (Pocket Books of New York, 1973).

Cruden's Compact Concordance, (Zondervan Publishing, 1968).

Dake, Finis Jennings, **God's Plan for Man** (Dake Bible Sales, Inc., 1949).

DeHann, Richard, **Good News for Bad Times** (Victor Books, 1975).

Eerdman's Handbook of the Bible (Lion Publishing, 1973).

Eyring, Dr. *Henry,* **The Faith of a Scientist** (Publishers Press, 1967).

Feingberg, Charles Lee, **Prophecy and the Seventies** (Moody Press, 1972).

Frankl, Viktor E., **Man's Search for Meaning** (Washington Square Press, 1969).

Green, Thomas Sheldon, M.A., **Greek/English Lexicon** (Zonervan Publishing, 1974).

Greene, Oliver B., **The Word Above All** (The Gospel Hour, 1971).

Hagin, Kenneth, **How Can You Know the Will of God,** (K. Hagin, 1972).

Halley, Henry H., **Halley's Bible Handbook** (Zondervan Publishing, 1965).

Kempis, Thomas, **Of The Imitation of Christ** (The New American Library, 1957).

Kenyon, E.W., **The Hidden Man** (Kenyon's Gospel Publishing, 1970).

LaHaye, Tim, **Transformed Temperments** (Tyndale House Publishing, 1975).

Lewis, C. S., **Mere Christianity** (MacMillan Publishing Co., Inc., 1960).

Lindsey, Hal, **There's A New World Coming,** (Vision House, 1974).

Little, Paul E., **Know Why You Believe** (Victor Books, 1973).

Malgo, Wim, **Israel's God Does Not Lie,** (The Midnight Call, Inc., 1972).

Martin, Walter R., **The Kingdom of the Cults** (1972).

Moody Monthly (April 1974).

Nettinga, James Z. Ph.D., **Quotations from the Bible** (American Bible Society, 1973).

New York Herald Tribune, "Is **Russia Set to Crack Iran?",** (1961).

Newsweek Magazine (November 19, 1973).

Otis, George, **The Solution to Crisis-America** (Bible Voice Distributing, 1972).

Ramm, Bernard, **The Christian View of Science and Scripture** (William Eerdman Publishing, 1971).

Pollock, John, **The Master-A Life of Jesus** (Victor Books, 1985).

Schweitzer, Albert, **The Quest of the Historical Jesus** (MacMillan Company, 1961).

Signs of the Times Magazine (January 25, 1843).

Smith, Hannah Whitall, **The Common Sense Teaching of the Bible** (Fleming H. Revell Co., 1985).

Strong, James, S.T.D., L.L.D., **The Exhaustive Concordance of the Bible** (MacDonald Publishing Co.).

These Times Magazines (March 4, 1974).

Thompson, Frank Charles, D.D., Ph.D., **The New Chain Reference Bible** (King James Version) (B.B. Kirkbridge Bible Company, Inc., 1964).

Time Magazine (March 4, 197 4).

Vine, W.E., M.A., **Expository Dictionary of New Testament Words** (Fleming H. Revell
Co., 1966).

Walvoord, John F., **The Nations in Prophecy** (Zondervan Publishing, 1978).

Wand, J.W.C., **A History of the Early Church to A.D. 500** (Methuen & Co., Ltd., 1974).

Wasserzug, Dr. G., Ph.D., **The Terrifying Goal of the Ecumenical Movement** (The Midnight Call, Inc., 1974).

Webster's New World Dictionary, College Edition.

Printed in the United States
By Bookmasters